C000109713

Paintings in Wood FRENCH MARQUETRY

Paintings in Wood

FRENCH MARQUETRY FURNITURE

Yannick Chastang

Yannick Chastang

Published by the Wallace Collection to accompany the exhibition *Paintings in Wood* held at the Wallace Collection, London from 4 October to 31 December 2001.

© The Trustees of the Wallace Collection 2001

All rights reserved. No part of this publication may be reproduced, stored in a retieval system, or transmitted, in any form or by any means, electronic, mechanical, photocopying, recording or otherwise, without the prior permission of the publisher.

ISBN 0 900785 66 7

Designed by Sally McIntosh
Printed by Westerham Press Limited

Wallace Collection photography by
Gordon and Simon Roberton and Richard Valencia

frontispiece
Detail of the floral basket marquetry on the lower door of the *secrétaire à abattant* by Jean-François Leleu, *c.*1772 (fig.35).

pages 12 and 13
Detail of a bearded mask on the front door of the cabinet-on-stand, attributed to André-Charles Boulle, *c.*1665-70 (fig.21). The mask is made of berberis and would originally have been a bright golden yellow.

Supported by the Michael Marks Trust

CONTENTS

ACKNOWLEDGEMENTS

The publication of this book was made possible by the support of the Michael Marks Trust and an anonymous donor; their generosity is greatly appreciated.

I am grateful to have had the opportunity to work with Peter Hughes, whose *Wallace Collection Catalogue of Furniture* was an invaluable resource, and would like to thank him, not only for the generous sharing of his many years of research, but also for his helpful suggestions regarding the text of this book. I am also fortunate to have been tutored some years ago by Pierre Ramond whose own publications on marquetry lead the field.

I would like to thank my many Wallace Collection colleagues who have assisted with this project. They include Rosalind Savill for her faith in and support of me, Jeremy Warren for his support and extensive editing of the text, Julia Parker for managing the book production, Paul Tear for his faith and practical support, David Edge and Stephen Duffy for advising on early versions of the text, Joanne Charlton and Emma Baudey for assistance with photographic material and Alastair Johnson for additional photography.

I am also indebted to individuals of other institutions who have shared their knowledge with me or who have provided photographic material: Carolyn Sargentson and Juliette Hibou of the Victoria and Albert Museum; David Wheeler of the Royal Collection; and Thierry Devynck of the Bibliotheque Forney. I am also grateful to Sir Geoffrey de Bellaigue and Christopher Payne for their advance reading of the text.

Above all, I would like to thank my wife and former colleague, Sharon Vincent Chastang for her considerable assistance in writing and editing the text. Her support and encouragement throughout this project has been incalculable.

Y ANNICK C HASTANG
Conservator, The Wallace Collection

PREFACE

Museums can be daunting places, filled with unfamiliar objects which at first sight may have little relevance to our lives. But are they really so unfamiliar? A grand and elaborate Louis XV *commode* is at the end of the day only a chest-of-drawers, no different in its original function from those we use every day at home. What makes it different and special are its destination – a discerning royal patron or member of the court – and its construction: made from exotic materials; fashioned by skilled craftsmen using intricate and ingenious techniques. If we try to look at our *commode* through the eyes of the cabinet-makers who made it, then some of our difficulties may disappear and unease give way to wonder. Understanding how an object was made is one important way in which it can more readily become a work of art to be admired and enjoyed.

Paintings in Wood opens a window onto one of the most intricate and fascinating aspects of the cabinet-maker's art – marquetry, the art of creating pictures and patterns through the inlaying of veneers of variously-coloured woods. Marquetry reached perhaps its greatest expression in the furniture made for the French court during the eighteenth century. There are few better places in the world than the Wallace Collection to study this furniture and, in consequence, the art of the *marqueteur*. Our remarkable furniture holdings include many royal pieces from the reigns of Louis XIV, Louis XV and Louis XVI, which are shown in Hertford House together with contemporary paintings, porcelain, metalwork and sculpture.

As a national museum, we aim to care for these wonderful and unique collections and to make them accessible to the public. I like to think that this book, which accompanies an exhibition at the Wallace Collection, helps us with both these tasks. Both book and exhibition owe their genesis to the important furniture conservation work carried out over recent years by the Wallace Collection's Conservation Department, under the guidance of our international advisory panel of experts. We cannot expect furniture which has survived for over two hundred years to look the way it did the day it was made, even less so when we learn that, in order to keep its vibrant colours fresh, Louis XV had to have the surfaces of his favourite pieces re-worked in his own lifetime. But modern conservation methods can help to stabilise these objects, so they remain available for future generations to enjoy, and also to restore clarity and even some colour to their beautiful surfaces. I hope you too will feel, as you turn these pages, that the eighteenth-century writer Savary des Brulons was not exaggerating when he described the finest marquetry designs of his time as akin to 'paintings in wood'.

ROSALIND SAVILL
Director, The Wallace Collection

INTRODUCTION

The study of French furniture has greatly improved over the last 50 years, access to archive material has never been better and the establishment of conservation as a profession has meant that objects are now looked at in a new light. Up until a few decades ago objects were restored by tradesmen, cabinet-makers, gilders and metal workers who used traditional techniques which were at times very intrusive. Also there was very little record keeping of the work carried out, or of what was found under the surface veneer.

Today, the study of French furniture is to a greater extent a partnership between curator and conservator, with on occasions some scientific input in the form of analysis of materials. Conservators seek to stabilise the condition of objects using minimal intervention techniques and to record their findings. During such treatment we can often get a better understanding of how objects were constructed and the techniques used to decorate them. By checking findings against original 18th-century sources we can start to build up a picture of the techniques and recipes used to create these wonderful objects.

This book, the first general survey of French marquetry to be written in English, covers the history, sources, materials, techniques and colours of marquetry and is the product of new research by the author and others. Recent conservation projects undertaken in the Wallace Collection Conservation Department, on many of which my colleague Yannick Chastang has worked, have contributed to the understanding of the various decorative techniques described in this book. The construction of reproduction marquetry panels for the associated exhibition has given the opportunity to try out some of the marquetry cutting techniques found on objects and described in 18th-century texts, to see if in reality they can be recreated.

The desire to decorate wood dates back over two thousand years. That desire continues today with modern furniture designers, cabinet-makers and marquetry cutters still producing modern marquetry, sometimes in the traditional way, sometimes using 'high tech' equipment such as lasers. This book will be a great asset to the study of marquetry and I hope it will inspire us all to look a little more carefully and with more understanding at these wonderful designs.

PAUL TEAR
Head of Conservation, The Wallace Collection

1   MARQUETRY TECHNIQUES

The woodworker's desire to decorate wooden objects is as old as
man's ability to work with wood. In discovering the potential of
wood for the creation of artefacts, early civilisations soon realised
that this material could also be exploited to add a decorative element.
In the earliest days, this was more likely to take the form of carving
or engraving, rather than the juxtaposition of woods of contrasting
colours. As a form of wood decoration, marquetry or inlay was initially
circumscribed by technical limitations, and thus its story comes to be
determined by the woodworker's ability to overcome these barriers.
Although ancient civilisations – notably the Egyptians, Greeks and
Romans – did come to develop sophisticated marquetry traditions,
knowledge of these survived the Dark Ages only through the
descriptions of writers such as Pliny. In marquetry, as in many other
art forms, the European Renaissance heralded not just a revival of
interest in the subjects of classical art, but also a rediscovery of
long-lost techniques. ❧

Figure 1
The Gubbio *studiolo* of
Federico da Montefeltro,
made between 1476 and
1482 by Italian craftsmen,
is one of the finest
surviving examples of
the marquetry technique
of *intarsia*.
THE METROPOLITAN
MUSEUM OF ART,
ROGERS FUND, 1939.
(39.153). PHOTOGRAPH
© THE METROPOLITAN
MUSEUM OF ART

Figure 2
This German match-lock target rifle, dated 1598, has a walnut stock, richly inlaid with stag-horn and stained ivory decoration using the *intarsia* technique. Engraving has been used to supply finishing touches and details.
THE WALLACE COLLECTION, INV. A1072

Figure 3
Detail of the front of the writing and toilet table *c.*1763-4 (fig.30). The marquetry comprises a geometrical parquetry pattern in kingwood, tulipwood and grey-stained sycamore.
THE WALLACE COLLECTION

Intarsia, or the primitive inlay technique

By the fourteenth century, Italian craftsmen had come to lead Europe in the art of marquetry decoration, demonstrating unrivalled skill in the creation of pictorial representations in wood through a marquetry technique known as inlay or *intarsia*. The basic technique of *intarsia* involved the use of a fairly primitive tool: an ordinary knife blade mounted on a handle which measured about 40 centimetres (18 inches) in length. This tool is called an inlay or shoulder knife. The knife was used by grasping the long handle with both hands and supporting the end of the handle on the shoulder. With the control afforded by this unique tool, master craftsmen could cut precisely shaped cavities in the solid wood of a piece of furniture or panelling and then fit into the cavity a piece of wood or other material of contrasting colour or grain, such as ivory, bone or horn. Artists including Giuliano da Maiano (1432-1491), his brother Benedetto (1444-1496), Fra Giovanni da Verona (1457-1525) and others whose names have been lost created remarkable *intarsia*, rare examples of which survive today in churches and museums. Most designs were rectilinear in style and amongst the most popular compositions were those which exploited the new understanding of perspective. These included the two *studioli* made for Duke Federico da Montefeltro. One, completed in 1476, remains *in situ* in the Palazzo Ducale in Urbino, whilst the second, once in the palace in Gubbio, has now been reassembled in the Metropolitan Museum of Art in New York (fig.1). Made between 1476 and 1482, the wood panelling of the Gubbio *studiolo* is designed to give the illusion of a room furnished with cupboards and tables. Some of these *trompe l'oeil* cupboards are open or ajar revealing a wide range of objects inside, including musical instruments, books and armour, in fact all the necessary accoutrements of the enlightened Renaissance man. Made of indigenous, local woods, both stained and in their natural colours, this panelling is breathtaking in its scope and accomplishment. Such heights of creativity could only be achieved with the support of a powerful patron such as Duke Federico.

While highly sophisticated patterns could be produced with the early techniques of *intarsia*, the use of a knife as the principal tool nevertheless limited significantly the craftsman's ability to produce more complex curves. A major development around the middle of the sixteenth century revolutionised *intarsia* work. This was the invention of a tool still in use today: the fret-saw, otherwise known as the piercing saw. A small metal frame-saw fitted with a fine blade which enables curved lines to be cut in diverse materials, the fret-saw gave the craftsman a whole range of new possibilities. Pieces of inlay could be cut with great accuracy, then inlaid into cavities created with the inlay knife, thereby allowing a greater flexibility and range of designs. By this time craftsmen were inlaying into veneered backgrounds which had been previously glued onto the furniture carcase, as well as into the solid carcase itself. It can be said that modern marquetry would never have existed without the invention of this tool.

The earliest representation of a fret-saw is in a marquetry panel made in around 1565, now in Ecouen, near Paris, where it is shown attached to the wall of a marquetry workshop. The complexity of *intarsia* work of the sixteenth century was directly related to the fineness of the fret-saw blade. It is no coincidence that some of the most accomplished sixteenth-century marquetry was produced in Augsburg, a city with a reputation for metalwork of the finest quality, the manufacture of which required extensive use of the piercing saw.

Many fine works of art made with this technique survive from this period, including furniture, gun stocks, panelling and other wooden artefacts. They include a German match-lock target rifle dated 1598 (fig. 2), its stock richly inlaid with stag-horn and stained ivory decoration. The intricate *intarsia* decoration on this weapon has been cut with a fret-saw and then inlaid into the solid walnut stock.

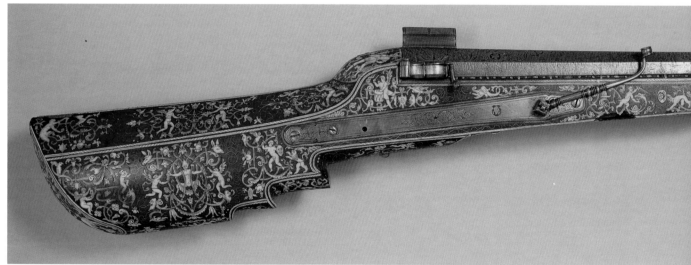

FIG 2

FIG 3

Parquetry, called *Tarsia Geometrica*

Parquetry is the simplest decorative veneer technique and the earliest known to have been used. It is still in use today. In its basic form, parquetry can be compared to mosaic work. Geometrical pieces of contrasting veneer are cut with a knife, a saw or a fret-saw and are then glued onto a solid wood base to form a surface decoration. Strictly speaking, parquetry is only made up of geometrical elements.

Boulle marquetry, called *Tarsia a Incastro*

The introduction of the fret-saw made possible the development of the Boulle marquetry technique, which has been used by many craftsmen since its creation at the beginning of the seventeenth century and is still in use today. Despite its name, the Boulle marquetry technique was invented some time around the

FIG 4

Figure 4

The subject of this late seventeenth-century *première-partie* Boulle marquetry panel, which has been reused on a nineteenth-century cabinet, is typically *Berainesque*.

THE WALLACE COLLECTION, INV. F17

1620s, well before André-Charles Boulle himself (1642-1732) was born. While it is now recognised that he did not invent the technique, he is generally credited with having developed it to new heights of refinement.

The Boulle marquetry technique is best known in relation to metals and turtle-shell. However, the earliest examples of Boulle marquetry make use of two contrasting materials such as woods, ivory, bone or turtle-shell. We do not know whether the development of the Boulle marquetry technique was in response to a new fashion for metal marquetry or if it was driven by technical developments. The inlay knife could not be used to work such newly fashionable hard materials as turtle-shell, ebony and metal. They could however be worked with the fret-saw, the result being the Boulle technique.

The easiest way to produce marquetry from hard materials was to cut simultaneously two contrasting veneered materials joined temporarily together, one on top of the other, in a sort of sandwich, called a packet. A drawing was made directly onto or otherwise glued onto the surface of this packet and the design was then cut out using a fret-saw. This produced two identically-shaped cut-out patterns, not dissimilar to jigsaws, in contrasting materials. The pieces of each 'jigsaw' were separated and reassembled using alternating colours to produce a piece of marquetry, which could either have a lighter design set against a dark background or a dark design against a light background. The combination of a dark background, usually of turtle-shell with the inset design in brass, or another light-coloured material, is called *première-partie* marquetry. A light background, usually in brass, with the inset design in turtle-shell is called *contre-partie* marquetry. This is illustrated by the pair of pedestals (*gaînes*) c.1700 where fig.5A shows *première-partie* marquetry of a brass design on a background of dark turtle-shell and fig.5B shows *contre-partie* marquetry of turtle-shell set against a brass background. The marquetry for the two stands would have been cut in one action. Throughout the eighteenth century, the cost of *contre-partie* marquetry was substantially lower than that of *première-partie*, by as much as twenty per cent.

The same principles were adopted by Boulle and his contemporaries for the making of floral marquetry. Boulle was a master of the art of creating flowers in marquetry, as can be seen from the cabinet-on-stand attributed to him and made *c.*1665-70 (fig.21). This cabinet was made using a derivation of the Boulle marquetry technique. Tracings or drawings of individual flowers and other decorative elements were transferred or glued onto the piece of wood selected for cutting. The *marqueteur* would cut along the lines of the drawing using a very fine fret-saw. The piece of wood to be cut was placed between the jaws of a foot-activated vice, to hold it firmly in place during the cutting process. This tool, which the *marqueteur* sits astride, is called a donkey. After cutting, the pieces of wood would next be shaded. Selected pieces of the flower design were placed in hot sand for a short period until the edges darkened, creating a shadow effect

FIG 5A

FIG 5B

which, once the marquetry was finished, would give depth to the floral composition. The shadowing stage is one of the most important elements in the process of making marquetry. Once all the shadows had been created, the numerous individual pieces of each flower were glued onto a paper backing to hold them in place. The resulting individual flowers were often prepared in advance and kept in boxes until needed for the next stage in the marquetry process. A catastrophic fire in Boulle's workshop in 1720 destroyed, amongst many other items, six chests-of-drawers containing ready-cut flowers.

When it came to fixing the floral decoration within the ebony background of the marquetry, using an inlay knife to excavate cavities would have been impractical as ebony is too hard, even in veneer form. The flowers and other elements forming the composition were therefore temporarily glued in place on top of the ebony veneer. The *marqueteur* would cut out around these with the fret-saw, creating holes of the exact shape and size in the ebony veneer. Each element of the design would be placed in its correct space and maintained in position using a paper backing, until the entire marquetry had been completed and could be finally glued onto the solid wood carcase of the furniture.

Once in its final position the marquetry would be finished. Scraping and sanding would remove irregularities, giving the marquetry an even surface and revealing the richness and colour of each material. Following this, the metal and turtle-shell would be engraved and the engraved lines filled with a black filler to make them stand out. Wood marquetry could also be engraved to provide added detail.

Simultaneous cutting of the veneers to be combined resulted in the permanent loss of a small amount of material along the cutting line; this gap would have to be filled with glue or filler. The resulting black line left around each cut element is the major disadvantage of the Boulle technique, and the reason why the technique was generally used with dark backgrounds, particularly ebony or turtle-shell, where the line does not show. Boulle is also one of the fastest marquetry techniques as more than one marquetry panel is produced at a time.

The advanced inlay technique

Although the Boulle technique was still being used, Parisian *marqueteurs* undertaking floral marquetry from the second quarter of the eighteenth century onwards used a different technique, which had its origins in *intarsia*. Literature on furniture manufacture techniques and, in particular, marquetry, is rare during the seventeenth century and for much of the eighteenth. However, during the second half of the eighteenth century many more books were written and published on these subjects. The cabinet-maker's craft was discussed in detail in Diderot's *Encyclopédie* of 1751-80 and in 1772 the carpenter André-Jacob Roubo published a major work on the subject, *L'Art du Menuisier*. Roubo's book remains

Figure 5

The predominantly turtle-shell pedestal above (A), is in *première-partie* marquetry whilst that below (B), with the ground in brass, is in *contre-partie* marquetry.

THE WALLACE COLLECTION, INV. F53-4

Figure 6

This painting of an English marquetry / cabinet-making workshop was made by the Swedish painter Martin Elias between 1768 and 1780. French workshops of the time would have been similar. The man in the foreground, seated on a marquetry donkey, cuts pieces of veneer with a fret-saw. The man working behind on the circular table uses a small inlay knife and hammer to create cavities in a background, into which he inlays the cut pieces of veneer.

THE SWEDISH NATIONAL ART MUSEUM, STOCKHOLM

the best and most comprehensive book on eighteenth-century cabinet-making, even though some modern cabinet-makers have criticised the fact that not all the recipes he quotes can be successfully replicated. Published during one of the richest periods of French marquetry, the techniques Roubo discusses include many of the most important used by eighteenth-century cabinet-makers and *marqueteurs*. He provides a detailed discussion of what may be called the advanced inlay technique.

This technique was used to produce the marquetry made by such master-craftsmen as Jean-Pierre Latz (*c.*1691-1754), Jean-François Oeben (1721-63), Jean-Henri Riesener (1734-1806) and Jean-François Leleu (1729-1807). Analysis and conservation work on furniture by these makers have revealed distinctive tool marks and outline drawings cut into the carcase below the marquetry. Further evidence of the use of this inlay technique is found in a painting representing an English marquetry workshop of the late eighteenth century. Executed by the Swedish painter Martin Elias during his travels in England between 1768 and 1780, the painting depicts a craftsman cutting a piece of wood with a fret-saw while another gouges out a cavity in a table top using a small inlay knife (fig.6). Although it is unlikely that all cabinet-makers in Paris in the eighteenth century used this technique, it is safe to assume that the majority did so. Many were of

FIG 6

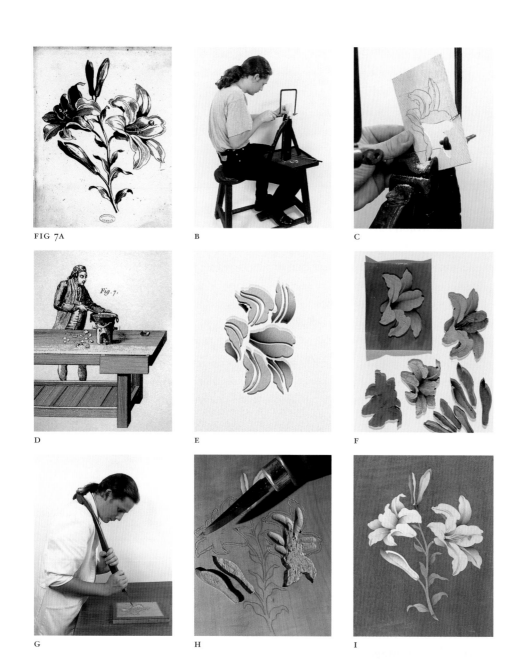

FIG 7A

B

C

D

E

F

G

H

I

FIG 8

Figure 7
The advanced
inlay technique:

A Engraving of lilies from
  *Le Livre de Principes de
  Fleurs* by Tessier
B Cutting the individual
  lilies with the fret-saw
  and donkey
C Close up view of B
D *Marqueteur* doing the
  shading (*L'Art du Menuisier*
  by Roubo)
E Individual lilies with
  shadow
F Lilies glued on a backing
  paper
G Inlay of elements into the
  background veneer using
  the shoulder knife
H Close up view of G
I The finished marquetry.

Figure 8
Detail of the back
marquetry of the roll-top
desk made by Riesener
for the comte d'Orsay,
*c.*1770 (fig.32), representing
a tied bouquet of lilies,
roses and other flowers
executed in the advanced
inlay technique.

THE WALLACE COLLECTION

foreign, particularly Flemish, origin. They lived and worked in the same area of Paris around the Faubourg Saint Antoine and undertook their apprenticeships in the same workshops. Despite the fact that this technique is closer to *intarsia* than to Boulle marquetry, this late eighteenth-century veneered decoration is also generally described as marquetry.

On the back of the roll-top desk (*bureau à cylindre*) made *c.*1770 for the comte d'Orsay (fig.8), Riesener has depicted a bunch of lilies taken directly from an engraving by Tessier. A modern reproduction of this detail has been made, using the technique described by Roubo, in order to illustrate the process. The *marqueteur* would have made a tracing of the Tessier engraving, copying the detail of each individual flower and leaf. Just as in the Boulle marquetry technique this tracing would have been transferred or glued onto a piece of veneer, which would then have been prepared in the same way. Again as with Boulle, a stock of ready-cut finished flowers would have been built up, the 1763 inventory of Oeben's workshop, for example, recording a chest of pre-cut marquetry flowers.

When a piece of furniture was to be veneered with floral decoration, the first stage would involve glueing a sheet of background veneer onto a completed solid wood carcase. A simple drawing of the final composition would then be outlined on the veneer to assist with the placement of the flowers and marquetry elements. The flowers and marquetry elements selected for the design would be placed on top of the background veneer and carefully marked out into the veneer using a scriber. Turning to his inlay knife, with its long handle mounted with a sharp blade, the *marqueteur* would cut deep into the background veneer along the scriber lines. This is the process which can create the distinctive marks on the solid wood carcase. The cut-out portion of the background veneer would then be removed, creating a cavity into which the marquetry elements would be fitted and glued. Each flower and other decorative element was individually inlaid using this technique.

The top of the piece of furniture would then be sanded, engraved if necessary, and a finish applied. Despite its time-consuming nature, this technique was preferred to the Boulle technique during the second half of the eighteenth century. Its advantages, besides those of technique, lay in the complete liberty of interpretation of the marquetry composition which it afforded the *marqueteur* and the exactness with which each marquetry element fitted into its space. A flower or leaf could easily be added or left out depending on the maker's whim. Such freedom allowed the resulting marquetry composition to be adapted, often superbly so, to the piece of furniture with its bronze mounts and other decorative features.

On the other hand, this technique only allowed one marquetry composition to be completed at a time. With intensive practice and long experience the eighteenth-century craftsmen produced high quality marquetry very quickly. However, the Industrial Revolution provided the impetus in the next century for the development of faster and cheaper techniques which would alter the course of standard marquetry practice. There are a few rare examples of nineteenth-century marquetry using inlay, but today the technique is virtually extinct.

The element by element approach, or modern marquetry technique

The element by element technique has been used since the nineteenth century. Its origins lie, firstly, in refinements to earlier marquetry techniques and, secondly, in more sophisticated tools, developed in particular during the Industrial Revolution. The technique allows for the making of up to twelve marquetry panels at one time.

Each element comprising a marquetry design still has to be cut individually but, with the more advanced tools available, up to twelve examples of the same element can be cut in one single action, by assembling twelve sheets of veneer in a single packet for the cutting process. The shading process in hot sand still has to be carried out separately on each piece. Once this stage has been completed, the elements of the flower or other design are assembled and inserted into the background veneer. They are maintained in place with a paper backing, before finally being glued onto the solid wood carcase of a piece of furniture. The background veneer sheets are cut using the same technique. This process encouraged the development of specialised marquetry workshops which produced ready-made marquetry and sold it on to cabinet-makers.

Most makers today still use this nineteenth-century technique, although more recently we have seen the introduction of the still expensive options of laser cutting and high pressure water cutting.

As new techniques are developed, the craftsman is able to choose from an ever wider range. A craftsmen may be more comfortable with an older technique if it produces the desired result, and so may decide to continue using it. It is dangerous therefore to attempt to date precisely when particular techniques first appeared and when they finally disappeared. It is certainly unrealistic to assume that all the cabinet-makers working at any given time would have been using exactly the same technology. The development of marquetry techniques must also be considered in the context of the technical advances in other industries directly related to that of marquetry. As an example, the rapid developments in metallurgy from the mid-eighteenth century onwards would have influenced marquetry techniques, because they facilitated greatly the manufacture of the small strips of steel used to make the blades for marquetry fret-saws.

Figure 9
Boulle marquetry technique:

A Drawing used as a source of decoration
B *Marqueteur* using the donkey and fret-saw for cutting (*L'Art du Menuisier* by Roubo)
C Cutting the tulips using the fret-saw
D The cut tulips and leaves
E Shading the tulip petals in hot sand
F A finished tulip glued on a backing paper
G Cutting of the background veneer to enable the insertion of the tulip
H Tulip ready to be placed in its ebony background
I The finished marquetry.

FIG 9A

B

C

D

E

F

G

H

I

2

MATERIALS USED IN MARQUETRY

Marquetry comprises shaped pieces of veneer assembled together to form a decorative pattern which is applied to the carcase of a piece of furniture. A veneer is a thin sheet of material which can be glued onto a wood surface. Alongside the development of marquetry technology, techniques such as sawing, hammering, rolling and slicing have been developed over the centuries for various materials, to enable the craftsman to create thin enough sheets of veneer. Most raw materials, ranging from organic matter such as wood, horn and bone to inorganic materials, such as metal or even stone, can be processed to obtain a thin veneer. However, not all these materials can be adapted to marquetry, as not all are suitable for use with a fret-saw or knife. Indeed, the fret-saw is only suitable for cutting relatively soft materials. The materials most commonly used by *marqueteurs* throughout the ages have been soft and hard woods, ivory, horn, bone, turtle-shell, and soft and medium-hard metals, such as brass or pewter. Some materials, including some very hard woods or the brittle mother-of-pearl, which might be thought to be too hard or fragile, have in fact been used successfully for isolated examples of marquetry, but this is very rare. ❧

Figure 10
Detail of the inside of a wardrobe attributed to Boulle, *c.*1700 with scrolling foliates of engraved pewter set into a background of ebony and reddish purpleheart.
THE WALLACE COLLECTION, INV. F62

Figure 11
Detail of the marquetry
on a wardrobe attributed
to André-Charles Boulle,
*c.*1700 made of blue-painted
horn background imitating
lapis lazuli with inlaid
scrolling brass foliates.
THE WALLACE COLLECTION,
INV. F62

In the case of some materials which would theoretically be highly desirable but which are quite unsuitable for working in this way, the *marqueteur* compensates by imitating them with substitutes. For example, painted horn is used to imitate lapis lazuli, a semi-precious stone too brittle and too hard to be commonly used in marquetry techniques. Blue horn imitating lapis lazuli can be seen used in conjunction with brass on the two Boulle wardrobes in the Wallace Collection (fig. 11). Whilst stone offers exciting potential in terms of colour and effect, and was used with great success in sixteenth-century Florence in the technique called *pietre dure,* it has been used since in marquetry only by a very few specialised craftsmen. Whilst *pietre dure* enjoyed considerable fame and popularity throughout Europe, the difficult nature of the raw materials hindered wider development of this painstaking technique. It was more practical for *marqueteurs* to focus on making marquetry using the flexible, softer materials available to them.

The rapid development, from the beginning of the seventeenth century onwards, of new styles of furniture was given an additional impulse by the introduction of new materials suitable for decorating furniture surfaces. The diversity of materials available from the beginning of the seventeenth century enabled marquetry to develop until it became the sophisticated technique seen in late seventeenth and eighteenth-century furniture. Before the expansion of trade routes, the only materials available to the *marqueteur* were those which could be found in his own country or region. Early marquetry work, such as *intarsia*, was usually made using a combination of indigenous woods and materials, such as horn and bone, which could be obtained inexpensively from local sources. European woods unfortunately have a very limited range of colours, restricting the palette of the *marqueteur* to a range of off-whites, yellows and browns. Even with a good knowledge of the whole range of wood species available, the early craftsmen generally had to rely on the quality of their drawing, on the technique of shadowing and, occasionally, on wood-dyeing. They could extend their range of effects by using different parts of the tree, exploiting variations in the fineness of the grain and in the colour, and also making use of the burr. Burr, the scar tissue formed by the tree, has always been highly-prized for its knotty decorative appearance. Finally, different examples of the same species of tree vary naturally in the colour or shade of their wood. Despite the

FIG 11

inherent limitations in the availability of raw materials early *intarsia* furniture was often surprisingly accomplished, demonstrating the excellent knowledge of materials among the best Renaissance craftsmen.

With the increase in international trade resulting from the Age of Exploration, fresh materials arrived which offered a completely new dimension to the art of the *marqueteur*. The new woods and materials, mainly from the East and West Indian trade routes, provided cabinet-makers with an extended palette of colours, many of which had not previously been available locally. Almost overnight the *marqueteur* had access to natural purples, reds, blacks and yellows. The growth in foreign trade also brought to Europe exotic dyes and stains which could be used where natural wood colour failed. Thus in the seventeenth century the *marqueteur* was able to create the colourful floral marquetry so fashionable at the time and could even approach, in his range of colours, those available to flower painters. *Marqueteurs* of the mid-eighteenth century were sometimes compared to painters, Savary des Brulons, author of the *Dictionnaire Universel de Commerce,* even according them the accolade of makers of *peinture en bois,* 'paintings in wood'.

Because of their superior range of colours and their versatility, the new woods and other materials came to be preferred to local materials. Tropical trees grow to proportions not witnessed in Europe, and the supply of exotic woods was seemingly inexhaustible. In *L'Art du Menuisier*, Roubo recommended them as being superior for use in marquetry, being of higher quality and possessing a wider range of colour.

The new materials were not simply superior, they were also endowed with an attractive exoticism and sense of novelty. The passion for ebony wood, which reached its height in the mid-seventeenth century, came about partly because, despite the large variety of species of trees in Europe, no living European wood approximated to it. Before the general availability of ebony, a black effect had instead to be obtained from bog oak which, being virtually rotten from long exposure to damp conditions, was fragile and impossible to polish. The uniquely high density of ebony results in a wonderful, polished material with an unequalled black colour, which must have seemed immensely exciting when it first appeared. Likewise, without the development of an import trade in turtle-shell, Boulle marquetry in the form we know it today might never have developed. Turtle-shell arrived in great quantities onto the French market as a by-product of the hunting and eating of warm-water sea turtles on voyages to and from India and the West Indies. The appeal of the exotic being what it is, it is worth considering whether perhaps turtle-shell would ever have become so desirable, were turtles to be found naturally in the Seine.

While the foreign materials were in many cases evidently superior to indigenous ones, the key factor restricting their universal use was their cost. We know from surviving inventories of seventeenth and eighteenth-century

following pages

Figure 12
Detail of Boulle marquetry
from the back panel of
the Four Continents clock
(fig.50).
THE WALLACE COLLECTION

workshops that only small quantities of exotic woods and materials were kept on the cabinet-maker's premises. Boulle's workshop inventory of 1715 and his compensation claim to the King, following the fire in his workshop in 1720, do not include any reference to turtle-shell and brass, somewhat surprisingly given the extensive use Boulle seems to have made of turtle-shell. It may be that the stocks of these materials were kept elsewhere. We know that Boulle and his sons managed to save some valuables from the flames, and perhaps he regarded his stocks of exotic materials as his first priority for rescue. Alternatively, this puzzling absence of turtle-shell in the workshop of one of the leading and most prolific cabinet-makers of the time may simply be explained by its cost. Without specific orders, cabinet-makers tended not to invest their limited working capital in materials. There is clear evidence of this fact from Madame de Pompadour's claim, following Oeben's death, to some mahogany wood in his workshop. She stated that she had already purchased this wood for it to be made into furniture for her. The thirty-four mahogany planks were valued at 1800 *livres,* which may be compared to the value of 240 *livres* placed on Oeben's horse. We know that the wood had been selected by Oeben himself, but in this and in many other cases the cost of the raw materials was so prohibitive that the customer had had to pay for them in advance.

Their high cost and the practical difficulty in obtaining many of these materials led to craftsmen developing techniques in which expensive materials were imitated by cheaper ones, as well as ever more refined techniques of cutting, aimed at minimising wastage. At the beginning of the seventeenth century, when the enormously expensive ebony was so sought after for the decoration of the most fashionable cabinets, unscrupulous cabinet-makers began to imitate ebony by developing improved techniques of dyeing cheap European woods. Woods such as holly, sycamore and pear wood, chosen for their dense grain, were left in a water-based solution of an exotic ground-wood powder which, through a second chemical reaction, dyed them black. The dense grain meant that, once polished, the wood could successfully simulate the best qualities of ebony. Imitations could be so convincing that from 1625, a strict regulation and control system was created in Holland in which genuine ebony furniture was stamped with a guarantee mark to distinguish it from the cheaper imitations. France on the other hand does not seem to have adopted any similar quality-control procedure. Black-dyed European woods had the further advantage that they were easier to work than the very hard, dense ebony. The tradition of using dyed European wood to imitate ebony, often with no intention to deceive, continued throughout the eighteenth and nineteenth centuries and is still in use today.

The following list, whilst not exhaustive, is aimed at providing the reader with the names and properties of some of the most commonly used materials in marquetry, together with information on how they would be prepared for use.

Materials used in the production of Boulle marquetry

The term 'Boulle marquetry' is used both for the technique and for the style. Although technically it can also refer to floral wood marquetry, here we will only discuss the foliate metal/turtle-shell marquetry most commonly associated with Boulle.

Turtle-shell, called tortoiseshell, (écaille de tortue)
Tortoiseshell is the common name given to the thin, translucent plates obtained from the carapace of the sea turtle. However, the *marqueteur* only used shell material from sea turtles, not from land tortoises, so it is more correct to use the term turtle-shell.

Turtle-shell is found on the upper body and on the plastron, or underside, of the turtle. It is a hard layer of shell formed on top of the reptile's bony outer shield. Three species of large marine turtles were most commonly used as sources for turtle-shell:
~ The green turtle *(chelone mydas), Franche*
~ The loggerhead turtle *(caretta caretta), Caouenne* or *Caouanne*
~ The hawksbill turtle *(chelone imbricata), Caret.*
Turtle-shell varies in colour and thickness depending on the species from which it derives and on the part of the turtle from which it is taken. The colour of turtle-shell from the upper body is generally amber to brown with patches of dark brown, while the turtle-shell taken from the plastron is a more even amber yellow. It is usually difficult to determine without scientific analysis the precise species from which turtle-shell used in Boulle marquetry has been taken. All these turtle species were hunted for their meat and all could be found in the warm seas around Africa, Asia and America, in particular around the Caribbean Islands, Madagascar, Indonesia and the Seychelles. The loggerhead and the hawksbill turtles produce a thicker shell than the green turtle and it seems probable that theirs were the preferred shells during the earliest period of production of Boulle furniture. The green turtle's shell became more

popular during the nineteenth-century Boulle revival in France since, being of a more even thickness, it requires less preparatory work

The plates taken from the upper body of the turtle have a slight convex shape while the plates from the plastron are flatter. It is usually possible to obtain thirteen workable plates from the upper body, all of which will differ in size depending on their place on the carapace. The plates are removed by boiling the bony carapace of the turtle. To prepare the shell for use in marquetry, the plates are first flattened using hot salt water and pressure. Both sides of the plate, particularly the exterior which has usually been damaged and scratched during the lifetime of the turtle, are scraped down and sanded to make the shell smooth and of even thickness. As turtle-shell plates are individually relatively small in dimension, they ideally need to be joined together to create the size of sheet needed for the marquetry panel. Pieces of turtle-shell can be welded together using moisture, heat and pressure. This technique was commonly used by makers of spectacles and toilet-wares in the nineteenth and twentieth centuries, as it enabled them to create blocks of turtle-shell from which they could carve out their products. The practice of welding together the shell for marquetry, which involves superimposing the prepared edges of two plates, is recommended as early as the eighteenth century. However, it seems that more commonly the *marqueteur* simply positioned different plates of turtle-shell next to each other, following the pattern of the shell, relying on the final glueing of the marquetry onto the piece of furniture to keep the pieces of shell joined.

The translucent properties of turtle-shell meant that the carcase material of the piece of furniture, usually oak or pine, would show through the clearer areas of the shell. To avoid this, a colour pigment was applied behind the shell. Some Boulle furniture has been found to have had a paper backing between the pigmented turtle shell and the carcase of the

furniture. Too often, insensitive earlier restoration work has destroyed the original pigment and the backing paper, with a modern pigmented glue being used to reapply the shell. In such cases it becomes difficult to know what colour was originally applied behind the turtle-shell. Roubo suggests that any colour may be used but states that black and red are most common. Recent scientific analysis has indicated that much turtle-shell marquetry furniture dating from the late seventeenth and the entire eighteenth century was pigmented with black, while red seems to have been preferred in the early seventeenth century and in the nineteenth-century Boulle marquetry revival. It has been argued that Boulle marquetry may have been developed in imitation of Japanese lacquer-work and, if so, the dark pigmentation behind the turtle-shell would have created a material with similar effects to lacquer.

All species of sea turtle are now protected. Over-exploitation, mainly for the manufacture of spectacles, for dressing table items and for food means that turtle-shell is today an extremely scarce commodity. Hunting of turtles has been banned and since 1993 only a few licensed conservators have been permitted to use old stocks of turtle-shell in their work.

Horn, (corne)

Cattle horn is a very versatile type of natural plastic, which has always been widely available in Europe. English horn was preferred for marquetry because it was reputedly more transparent. Thin sheets of horn are obtained by making an elliptic cut along the conical horn. The horn can then be opened and flattened using heat and moisture. Once flattened, the resulting thick plate of horn is cut or sliced into thinner sheets which are then scraped down and polished. The outer layers of horn tend to be less transparent, with more white markings than those further in, so as a result the purer inner layers are more sought after. Pieces of horn can be welded together using heat and moisture, but a simple clean straight or curving join is often preferred by the *marqueteur*. Pigment and paper are applied to the back of the horn sheets in the same way as with turtle-shell. In the seventeenth and eighteenth centuries blue and green were the preferred colours for use with horn, rather than the black or red commonly used with turtle-shell. Blue pigmentation could imitate lapis lazuli and green, malachite. Horn has also been used to imitate turtle-shell, chemical processes helping to create similar brown markings. However, the white markings commonly found in thin sheets of horn limited its versatility as a cheap replacement for turtle-shell since, even with a dark pigmentation, they were still visible.

Figure 13
Sea turtle from *L'Encyclopédie* by Diderot and d'Alembert

Figure 14
Front marquetry of a small casket, *c.*1715-20 (fig.54). The centre marquetry representing *chinoiserie* figures in a landscape setting, is made from a background of dark brown turtle-shell with engraved brass figures, trees and buildings surrounding a lake of mother-of-pearl with engraved waves. The marquetry panel is framed by bands of horn painted green contained within brass borders.
THE WALLACE COLLECTION

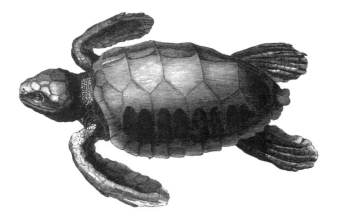

Brass, (laiton or cuivre jaune)

Brass is a yellowish composite metal, an alloy made predominantly of the red metal copper with small additions of the grey metal zinc. The exact composition of the alloy varies dramatically from one piece to another since before the nineteenth century the science of alloys was still very primitive. Thin brass sheets about one millimetre thick were required for marquetry. These were first produced by hammering flat a small block of brass, resulting in a relatively uneven sheet of small dimensions. Rolling technology was later developed which made possible the faster manufacture of larger and more even plates. The earlier small hammered brass sheets needed more preparatory work to make them suitable for use in marquetry. Small plates were joined together with a clean join which was often disguised or hidden beneath the bronze mounts of a piece of furniture. The side of the brass sheet that was to be glued onto the carcase of the piece of furniture was sometimes planed with a toothing plane, providing a regular grooved surface which would facilitate the sheet's adhesion when glued. The quality of the brass used was important, since hair-line cracks and other irregularities would prevent the marquetry taking a good polish once finished. As brass is a relatively hard material, the sheet was generally heated until it was red hot and then left to cool, in a process called annealing. This process would soften the brass, facilitating its preparation and the cutting of the marquetry.

FIG 14

Copper, (cuivre rouge or rosette)

Copper, a metal of a pinkish-red colour, is easier to work than brass. Although less commonly used than brass, it can occasionally be found in marquetry. Thin plates or sheets of copper were prepared for marquetry in the same way as brass.

Pewter, (étain)

An alloy of tin and lead with a grey-silver colour, pewter is common in Boulle marquetry. It is sometimes combined with brass and turtle-shell but, most commonly and felicitously, with blue horn, purpleheart or ebony. Unfortunately it easily oxidizes to a dull grey, a process which often happens as a result of contact with air or the acidic oak carcase of the piece of furniture.

The exact composition of the pewter used varies considerably to the extent that sometimes pure tin replaces pewter. These variations may have resulted from attempts to limit the oxidation process which occurs because of the lead content of the pewter. Depending on its content, pewter is a relatively malleable alloy. It was prepared in the same way as brass or copper, but because of its greater malleability, the rolling of pewter certainly predated that of copper and its alloys.

Mother-of-Pearl, (nacre)

Mother-of-pearl is obtained from sea shells. Numerous varieties can be used, each offering a variety of colours and texture. The most prized mother-of-pearl is white and translucent. It is cut into small pieces and is then sanded flat. The curved shape of the shell determines the size of the piece obtained, often no more than two centimetres (¾ inch) square. Mother-of-pearl is a hard, brittle material which is difficult to work with and the use of which was therefore very limited. It was often used to represent water in marquetry, for example, on a Boulle casket of *c.*1715-20 (fig.14) or the marquetry top of a knee-hole writing-table *c.*1715, (THE WALLACE COLLECTION, INV. F58).

Figure 15
The right-hand marquetry of a work-table stamped J-F Oeben, *c.*1765-70, made of flowers and details in sycamore, fruitwoods, holly and berberis, with the leaves and branches in stained sycamore. The marquetry is inlaid into a background of stained sycamore and framed with a border of tulipwood.
THE WALLACE COLLECTION, INV. F311

Berberis

Sycamore

Tulipwood

Black stained sycamore

Fruitwood

Materials for wood marquetry

Wood is the predominant material in the art of marquetry. Cabinet-makers had access to thousands of different species of wood and exploited the potential of many of them. The size of the tree is not a limiting factor for marquetry, so the variety of species which could be used was enormous. Identification of the woods used in a piece of marquetry can be very difficult for furniture scholars, not only because of the numerous species used, but because individual pieces of wood in the marquetry can be very small. Scientific analysis to distinguish one type of wood from another and the classification of the different species did not commence until the nineteenth century.

The preference of the *marqueteur* for one piece of wood over another depended primarily on its colour. If he could not obtain the right natural colour, he would obtain it by dyeing, the two missing colours in natural wood being green and blue. His choice might also be influenced by the effect of the grain, the visible marks of the tree's growth. The colour of the wood was so important to marquetry that Roubo classified woods firstly by their alphabetical names, as in most encyclopedias, but secondly, by their colours. As a second requirement, the chosen woods had to be hard enough to be satisfactorily polished once the marquetry had been finished.

Given the difficulties encountered in identifying wood today, it is somewhat reassuring to know that even the best cabinet-makers in the eighteenth century were sometimes confused about which wood they were working with. The wardrobe with a clock of 1715, attributed to Boulle (THE WALLACE COLLECTION, INV. F429), has a panel of dark black wood set next to a more purple wood. To the modern viewer this inconsistency is disturbing, yet below the bronze mounts of this door, where they have been protected from the light, the two different woods are equally black. Over time, the rosewood has discoloured more than the ebony, but presumably the maker was unable at the time to distinguish between the black ebony and the dark purple rosewood.

Confusion also abounds in the names used by the eighteenth-century French cabinet-makers. Woods were commonly given names according to their defining characteristics. Distinctively-coloured woods were given names such as purpleheart and *bois de rose* (or tulipwood). Exotic woods were universally and indiscriminately known in France since the seventeenth century as *bois des Iles*. It was common for different craftsmen to use different names for exactly the same wood. Roubo lists certain species of wood more than once under different names.

All woods used in marquetry have to be properly dried, then cut into thin sheets of veneer and, when necessary, dyed. In the early days of cabinet-making, when preparation of the log took place in the workshop rather than in a specialised shop, this would have been done by hand-sawing. Even though mechanical saw mills existed by the eighteenth century, most French cabinet-makers continued to cut their own veneers.

The following list is a selection of the most widely used woods in marquetry.

Ebony, (dyospiros, ébène)
Ebony (fig.16A) is one of the most important woods in the history of French cabinet-making. Its name is the source of the French term for cabinet-maker: *ébéniste*. In cabinet-making the name ebony is generally given to any wood of dense black colour, whatever the real botanical species. During the seventeenth century, the main sources of ebony were Madagascar and its surrounding islands, southern India and the east coast of Africa. True ebony varies in colour from a uniform dark black, to black with dark brown stripes. Seventeenth-century cabinet-makers had access to at least three or four types of

black wood, called ebony, but they commonly used a wood called Mozambique ebony. More dark purple than black, it is not from the real ebony species, *dyospiros,* but is in fact from the rosewood family, the *dalbergia.* Further ebony woods were discovered during the course of the nineteenth century.

Real ebony can be seen, used as a background veneer to the floral marquetry, on the cabinet-on-stand attributed to Boulle, *c.*1665-70 (fig.21). It was also commonly used as a border adjoining Boulle marquetry of metal and turtle-shell. Ebony is brittle, difficult to work with and produces an irritating dust. These reasons, as well as that of cost, meant that where the richness of the ebony was not considered essential, dyed woods were used as replacements. Such dyed woods are not only found on cheaper pieces of furniture. For example, Boulle's 1715 wardrobe with a clock (THE WALLACE COLLECTION, INV. F429) is made predominantly of real ebony, but uses dyed wood for the less prominent upper parts. Many of the marquetry works by Oeben, Riesener and Leleu make use of dyed wood, usually holly or sycamore, when a dark black wood is required for border strips or small floral details.

Figure 16
Woods used in the production of marquetry:
A Ebony
B Purpleheart
C Tulipwood
D Kingwood

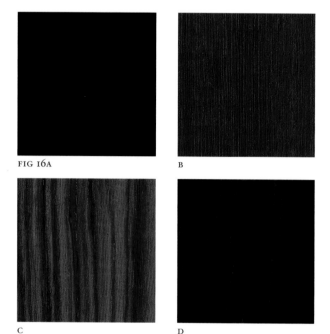

FIG 16A   B

C   D

Purpleheart, (peltogyne venosa, amarante)
Purpleheart (fig.16B) has a vibrant, and somewhat gaudy, bright and even purple colour that over time discolours to dark brown. The tree grows in South America and was exported to Europe from Guyana and Brazil. No wood with a similar purple colour can be found in Europe, so purpleheart has always been highly prized. Its unique colour is useful in floral marquetry, many of the flowers in the Boulle cabinet-on-stand (fig.21) being made of it. In the late seventeenth century, it was often combined with pewter and ebony in scrolling foliate marquetry, for example that inside the wardrobes by Boulle of *c.*1700 (fig.10). Purpleheart remained fashionable when marquetry declined in popularity during the early part of the eighteenth century, with some

furniture being veneered entirely with it. The contrast between the purple and the gold of the gilded bronze mounts would have been dramatic.

In the latter half of the eighteenth century, purpleheart came to be used, not so much for floral details, but more as a border for marquetry panels. Virtually all Oeben, Riesener and Leleu pieces, decorated with floral marquetry or with repetitive patterns, are veneered with a border of purpleheart. See for example the secretaire from 1780 (fig.38) or the comte d'Orsay's desk (fig.32), both by Riesener, and Leleu's secretaire of c.1772 (fig.35).

Tulipwood, (dalbergia decipularis, bois de rose)
Tulipwood (fig.16C) has a very attractive pink-yellow colour with pronounced stripes of violet-red and salmon-pink. Discoloured tulipwood is more even in colour, being a clear brown colour with fewer stripes visible. The tulipwood tree grows only in Brazil.

Tulipwood became fashionable from the first quarter of the eighteenth century and remained in vogue until the advent of plain-veneered mahogany furniture towards the end of the century. Although rarely used for floral details, tulipwood has played a major role in parquetry, being commonly used in conjunction with kingwood, purpleheart and *satiné* (or bloodwood). During the period of revival of floral marquetry in the 1740s, tulipwood was often used as a background. Most furniture in the Wallace Collection dating between the 1740s and the end of the 1770s includes some tulipwood veneer. The borders of the panels of marquetry and parquetry on the toilet and writing table of c.1763-64 (fig.30) are just one example.

Kingwood, (dalbergia cearensis, bois de violette)
Kingwood (fig.16D) has a naturally rich violet colour with stripes of dark brownish-violet. It also comes from Brazil and is from the same family as tulipwood. Once discoloured, it can be difficult to distinguish from tulipwood.

In the 1730s and 1740s, kingwood was extensively used for parquetry, in conjunction with *satiné* and tulipwood. The chest-of-drawers *(commode)* by Gaudreaus in the Wallace Collection (fig.25) of 1739, is mostly veneered with kingwood. The rich violet of the kingwood placed adjacent to the rich red of the *satiné* was intended to set off the gilt bronze on such heavily mounted commodes. Today the light brown striped wood is a pale reflection of its glorious original colour. During the revival of floral marquetry in the 1740s, kingwood was the wood most commonly chosen for the stylised flowers, which are made of end-grain veneer. Using the end-grain produces an even more striped and intense violet than ordinary long-grain kingwood, and the contrast between this and the background of tulipwood or *satiné* would have been very striking. The stylised flowers in the marquetry on the two sides of the filing cabinet by Latz, c.1750 (fig.26) are made of kingwood and are inlaid into a *satiné* background.

Bloodwood, (brosimum rubescens, satiné)
Bloodwood (fig.17A), called *satiné* in French, is generally wrongly translated into English as satinwood. Satinwood is in fact a bright yellow wood used extensively for late eighteenth-century English furniture. Bloodwood has rarely been used by English cabinet-makers, so nowadays the French name *satiné* is usually preferred to bloodwood in English as well.

Satiné comes from the South American tropical forests and, in particular, from Brazil, and is one of the deepest red woods available. It varies in hue from a deep, uniform red to a more striped wood with regular, even stripes of dark and lighter reds. These stripes catch the light differently depending on its source, so that a stripe which appears to be dark red when the light is coming from one side could look completely different when light falls on it from another direction. The differing reflections and modulations of the light are reminiscent of the effect of light on silk satin fabric, from whence derives the wood's name in French. With age, *satiné* darkens to a brownish-red, but the effect of rippling light against the grain can still be observed. *Satiné* was appreciated for floral marquetry details in the seventeenth century and can be seen used on the Boulle cabinet-on-stand of *c.*1665-70 (fig.21). As previously discussed, *satiné* was often used during the second quarter of the eighteenth century in conjunction with tulipwood or kingwood, for example on the sides and centre parquetry panels of the Gaudreaus commode of 1739 (fig.25). The squares of these parquetry panels are made of *satiné* with a grille of kingwood. Although the red of the *satiné* is now lost, its stripes are still visible.

Satiné remained popular with French cabinet-makers until the advent of the age of mahogany. Furniture of the 1730s and 1740s was often veneered in *satiné* on the outside, whilst furniture from the third quarter of the eighteenth century more commonly made use of this wood for the interior. The wood was relatively expensive and was primarily used as a veneer. However, the drawers inside the secretaire by Leleu of *c.*1772 (fig.36) are entirely made from solid *satiné*.

Sycamore or great maple,
(acer pseudoplatanus, érable sycomore)
Sycamore (fig.17B) is one of the most versatile and widely-used European woods for marquetry. A common European wood, it was considerably cheaper than its exotic counterparts. Sycamore is a creamy-white wood and is often used for making white flowers. It absorbs dyes easily and, once coloured, is very useful as a replacement for more exotic woods. The green leaves in floral marquetry are often made of dyed sycamore. It is also commonly dyed blue for flowers and skies, for example in the landscape marquetry of the drop front on the Foullet secretaire of *c.*1777 (fig.37). The original blue dye in this marquetry has discoloured with age and now appears green.

By the late 1750s, dyed sycamore had become highly fashionable as a marquetry background. Originally it seems most commonly to have been dyed a silver-grey colour, although today it has taken on a greenish tobacco colour. The Leleu secretaire (fig.35) is a good example of the use of grey sycamore as a background for each of the marquetry compositions. The sycamore pieces preferred for marquetry were those which had a natural sort of ripple effect due to stripes in the grain of the wood catching the light in different ways. Dyed grey sycamore is called harewood in English, while the French call it *gris satiné,* in reference to its similarities to *satiné* wood and satin silk.

Holly, (ilex aquifolium, houx)
Holly (fig.17C) is another white European wood which is used in the same way as sycamore. Used in marquetry throughout the ages, it is often difficult to distinguish from sycamore as both woods turn a creamy white with time. Holly is a purer white than sycamore and was the preferred choice when a pure white colour was required in marquetry. Holly can be dyed most colours, and small pieces of it were often dyed black to imitate ebony. Virtually all the white and black border strips framing marquetry from the second half of the eighteenth century are made of natural white and dyed black holly.

Fruitwood, (bois fruitiers)
The term fruitwood embraces many species including pearwood (fig.17D), applewood, and the wood of the whitebeam tree *(sorbus)*. It is difficult to distinguish one fruitwood from another and this general name is accordingly applied to woods with a dense, fine grain and a pinkish-brown colour. Pearwood and whitebeam have been greatly appreciated by the *marqueteur* throughout history and can be found as a component of most of the floral and trophy marquetry of the seventeenth and eighteenth centuries. Fruitwoods, too, were commonly dyed black in imitation of ebony.

Boxwood, (buxus sempervirens, buis)

Boxwood (fig. 17E) is a very dense wood with a pearl-yellow colour. It is a native of southern Europe. The density of boxwood makes it suitable for carving but not for dyeing. It seems to have been rarely used in eighteenth-century marquetry, but is more often found on nineteenth-century copies. The yellow colour is similar to old and discoloured natural sycamore and holly, and to some fruitwood. Nineteenth-century copies replicated eighteenth-century marquetry in its nineteenth-century condition, with boxwood often being used to imitate these discoloured woods. Boxwood and ebony, rather than white and black-dyed holly, are generally used for border strips on nineteenth-century reproductions.

Berberis or Barberry, (berberis vulgaris, épine-vinette)

Berberis (fig. 17F) is a small shrub that grows in most temperate climates and has been extensively used by *marqueteurs*. The roots of this shrub are highly-prized for their bright, intense yellow colour, which is unequalled even by exotic woods. The sawdust and shavings from berberis can even be used to stain other woods yellow as they contain a dyeing substance called berberine. Berberis shrubs were considered liable to parasites and so were systematically removed from crop fields as early as the seventeenth century, yet the wood remained highly fashionable and widely-used by French cabinet-makers. Most of the yellow flowers in marquetry by Boulle, Oeben, Riesener, Leleu and others are made of berberis. On the marquetry trophy on the drop front of the Leleu secretaire (fig. 35) the small compass is made of berberis, simulating brass.

Figure 17

Woods used in the production of marquetry:

A Bloodwood
B Sycamore
C Holly
D Fruitwood
E Boxwood
F Berberis

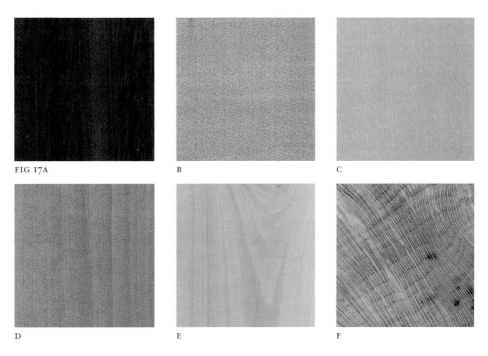

FIG 17A   B   C

D   E   F

3

THE BOULLE FAMILY AND THE
BEGINNINGS OF CABINET-MAKING IN FRANCE

Cabinet-making in sixteenth-century and seventeenth-century France
It is interesting to note that despite the dissemination of *intarsia* all
over Europe there is little surviving evidence of the use of *intarsia* in
France in the fifteenth and sixteenth centuries. Crafts in France had
been governed since the Middle Ages by a rigid guild system. The
traditionalism of the guild regulations resulted in the slowing down, and
even prevention, of the introduction of new styles and techniques. The
slow development of *intarsia* work in France was probably a casualty of
a stifling political and cultural atmosphere. François I (reigned 1515-47)
had invited Italian artists to work in France, particularly at Fontainebleau.
The accession to the French throne of Henri IV (reigned 1589-1610),
coinciding with a return of political and economic stability, resulted in
a policy of limiting the importation of luxurious objects by encouraging
foreign craftsmen to settle in France. These craftsmen, mainly from the
Low Countries and Germany, were the first to develop marquetry
techniques in France and they led the way in designing and making
the newly-fashionable cabinets. ໒

Figure 18
Detail from a front drawer
of the cabinet-on-stand
attributed to André-Charles
Boulle, *c.*1665-1770 (fig.21).
THE WALLACE COLLECTION

The ebony cabinet

In the early seventeenth century fashion and taste began to favour a new type of decorated cabinet, particularly in those countries enjoying direct access to the new exotic materials then arriving in Europe. The Dutch East India Company was created in 1602, whilst in the fifteenth and sixteenth centuries Portugal and Spain had developed extensive trade connections with South America and with the East Indies. The material which was to have the biggest impact on furniture design was the imported black hardwood known as ebony. In the earliest years of the seventeenth century, cabinets were often simply veneered with thick expensive ebony, which was then carved or engraved and partitioned with ripple mouldings to provide the decoration. The cabinet form was to provide a vehicle for the development of new types of marquetry.

As the style and form of the cabinet developed so did the type of joinery work necessary for its construction. Indeed, a new form of carpentry slowly emerged which was distinct from that practised by the common joiner making solid wood furniture. In the early seventeenth century those joiners who inlaid their cabinets with exotic materials such as ivory, turtle-shell and ebony came to be called cabinet-makers, or *menuisiers en ébène* (carpenters in ebony). While the name *ébéniste* was not officially adopted by the guild of carpenters / joiners until 1743, when it is first mentioned in a guild document, the specialism of the work was recognised much earlier.

Figure 19

The *Endymion Cabinet* was made in Paris *c*.1640-50. It has a solid wood carcase of pine and oak over which is laid a thick ebony veneer finely carved with a variety of allegorical scenes. Once open, the cabinet reveals a surprisingly rich and colourful interior with geometrical marquetry of various exotic woods.

COURTESY OF THE TRUSTEES OF THE VICTORIA AND ALBERT MUSEUM / PHOTOGRAPHER: P. BARNARD

Figure 20
This small cabinet-on-stand is thought to have been made by Pierre Gole for Henrietta Anne, duchesse d'Orléans, (1644-1670), daughter of Charles I of England. Its pine carcase is veneered with ivory, turtle-shell and a floral marquetry made from various woods and stained ivory and horn.

COURTESY OF THE TRUSTEES OF THE VICTORIA AND ALBERT MUSEUM / PHOTOGRAPHER: P. BARNARD

André-Charles Boulle (1642-1732)

André-Charles Boulle is perhaps the most famous cabinet-maker of all time. Born in Paris, he was himself a second-generation immigrant. His father, Jean Bolt, moved to Paris from Holland, where he had been born in 1610. Jean Bolt is known to have been in Paris before 1637, when he is recorded as working for the widow of the cabinet-maker Jean Senapre, who may himself have been a German immigrant. In the years that followed, Jean Bolt set up his own workshop and gradually changed his name to Jean Bould, and then finally to the form recognised today, Jean Boulle. While no furniture survives which can be definitely attributed to Jean Boulle, we know that André-Charles must have been present from an early age in the workshop of his father, as he was registered as a master in the guild of cabinet-makers before he was twenty-five years old. Following the death of the cabinet-maker Jean Macé in 1672, the powerful minister Jean-Baptiste Colbert (1619-1683) recommended Boulle to Louis XIV as the most skilful cabinet-maker in Paris and Boulle was given Macé's royal furniture workshop in the Louvre. This is a remarkable tribute to a man of only thirty years of age, at the beginning of his career. Occupying the Louvre royal workshop did not restrict Boulle to working exclusively for the King, and his talent was quickly recognised all over Paris. Louis XIV himself, however, still preferred the work of other cabinet-makers such as the Dutch immigrant Pierre Gole (c.1620–1684), the Italian Dominique Cucci (c.1640–1705) and Auburtin Gaudron (active c.1670-1713). It was only in 1700, after twenty-eight years working in the royal workshop for the aristocracy and the King's family, particularly the Grand Dauphin, that Boulle was finally to deliver a wardrobe made for the King himself. Boulle's workshop produced a wide range of objects, including not only furniture but also works in bronze and marquetry floors (none of which has survived). He is most celebrated, of course, for the type of marquetry in metal and turtle-shell which bears his name.

Figure 21

Cabinet-on-stand, with floral marquetry of various colourful exotic and indigenous woods against a background of black ebony, attributed to André-Charles Boulle, *c.*1665-1770.
THE WALLACE COLLECTION, INV. F16

The cabinet-on-stand continued in fashion for the first half of Boulle's working life. By this time the fashion was for cabinets decorated in floral wood marquetry on a dramatic black, or sometimes white, background. Gole, who was twenty years older than Boulle, with a workshop under royal patronage located in the Gobelins, was Boulle's closest competitor. Surviving pieces by Gole, such as a small rectangular cabinet on a six-legged stand decorated in floral marquetry on an ivory background, now in the Victoria and Albert Museum, show his work to have been enormously accomplished (fig. 20). There is evidence that Boulle and Gole both worked on the same furnishing project for the apartments of the Grand Dauphin at Versailles and undoubtedly Boulle was influenced by him.

Cabinet by André-Charles Boulle, 1665-70 (fig. 21)
Amongst the early works of Boulle is this cabinet-on-stand with floral marquetry and Boulle marquetry, dating from around 1665-70. Although many other cabinet-makers of the time worked in a similar style to Boulle this cabinet, together with four similar cabinets of the same period attributed to Boulle, now in other collections, are regarded as some of the finest works of their time. Despite a few alterations to the lower part, the Wallace Collection cabinet retains much of its original splendour. In both form and decoration it is a descendant of earlier ebony cabinets, retaining the same basic structure and a background of ebony. Its Baroque character is exemplified by the exuberant decoration, the prominent carved half-figures of Summer and Autumn (which may originally have been white) with their flowing draperies which constitute the cabinet's front legs, the monumentality of the architectural form, and the prominent central bronze trophy. The carving and moulding in the earlier ebony cabinets are succeeded by vibrantly-coloured marquetry decoration which, despite being mainly of floral subjects, does not compromise or lessen the overall impression of grandeur. Even though much of the marquetry decoration has suffered from discoloration by sunlight and from deterioration of the unstable dyes used to stain some of the woods, the extremely high quality of the floral marquetry remains evident. For example, the contrast of the foliage and flowers set into a dark ebony background is still dramatic, even though the original dynamic red, purple, white, yellow and green colours have been largely lost. As with most furniture, the decoration has responded to changes in fashion before the structure and, when looked at closely, it can be seen that this piece is a mixture of both the conservative and the avant-garde. Despite producing individual flowers which are almost perfect in their botanical details, Boulle has set them into a characteristically Baroque composition. The front centre panel, for example, displays the classical ornamentation expected from a Baroque piece, with at the bottom of the panel a mask and above that a scallop shell and scrolling forms leading into acanthus leaves. The large acanthus leaves serve as a frame or vase for the bouquet of flowers in the top half of the panel. Compared

Figure 22
Detail of marquetry table top from side table *c*.1705, attributed to André-Charles Boulle (fig.23).
THE WALLACE COLLECTION

to the formality of these classical motifs, the profusion of naturalistic flowers erupting into the space is quite stunning. There is even a naturalistic twisted ribbon at the top of the front centre panel, a motif which will be taken up in many marquetry compositions during the next century. Boulle's compositions anticipate the marquetry designs of the eighteenth century, when the acanthus leaves which hold the flowers together will be replaced by baskets or urns and the twisted ribbon will be used to tie the flower stalks together. Panels on the lower front and on the two sides, while similar in design to this central panel, are subtly different. Leaves and flowers on the ten drawer fronts are employed in double flower-spray designs which at first glance look formalised, but turn out not to be. The leaves are drawn from various botanical sources and there are many different varieties of flowers. The naturalistic flowers are individually clearly identifiable, and include narcissi, peonies, roses and honeysuckle. The incredible variety in the design of the flowers means that it is virtually impossible to find any flower-shapes which have been repeated. Whimsical touches such as the two grasshoppers, a bee and a beetle enforce the illusion of the garden transported indoors. The seventeenth century witnessed an influx of new species of flowers into Europe, the popularity of depictions of flowers in all art forms mirroring a new interest in botany. The profusion and abundance of nature in painting and marquetry coincided with a fashionable interest in the garden, but it was nature controlled and made perfect. The cabinet was created in an era in which the garden was the preserve of the rich and where a flower could become the world's most expensive commodity. During tulipomania only thirty years earlier in 1634-37, the price of a single tulip bulb had reached the equivalent of fifteen years salary for an average Amsterdam artisan.

This cabinet, however, contains little marquetry of the type with which Boulle's name would become synonymous. Boulle marquetry in its commonly understood form, in which metals and turtle-shell are combined, can be seen running along the horizontals of both the upper and lower parts, whilst patterns of stylised foliage create a strong vertical definition separating the centre panel from the drawers. All the marquetry panels are surrounded with an inlaid pewter strip. The gilt-bronze mounts, which would become ever more important in Boulle's later work, already begin to challenge their useful purpose by becoming ever more decorative (some or all of the keyhole escutcheons are probably later additions). The combination of bronze, pewter, ebony and highly coloured woods must have made this a truly glittering piece when it was first completed.

Boulle marquetry

It took several decades for taste to move from furniture decorated primarily with wood marquetry to furniture in which equal amounts of wood and Boulle marquetry are used for the surface decoration and, finally, to furniture entirely covered in brass, turtle-shell and gilded bronze mounts. The gilt and silver

highlights of metal furniture had the happy effect of reflecting candle light and it is perhaps not surprising that this bright metal furniture should have become very popular among those who could afford it.

By 1700 marquetry in metal and turtle-shell had become highly fashionable. Boulle himself was the pre-eminent master of this technique and the Wallace Collection is fortunate in possessing one of the finest collections in the world of furniture attributed to Boulle. The products of Boulle's workshop may be considered superior to those of other makers, not only because of the exceptional ability of the master in terms of the design, creation and quality of the marquetry, but also because of the quality and coherence of his bronze mounts, which give his furniture and his marquetry a quite unique dimension. Because Boulle worked in the Louvre he enjoyed protection from the strict guild regulations which obliged craftsmen to stay within the boundaries of their own specialism. The guild regulations prohibited the cabinet-maker from making his own bronze mounts despite the fact

FIG 23

FIG 24

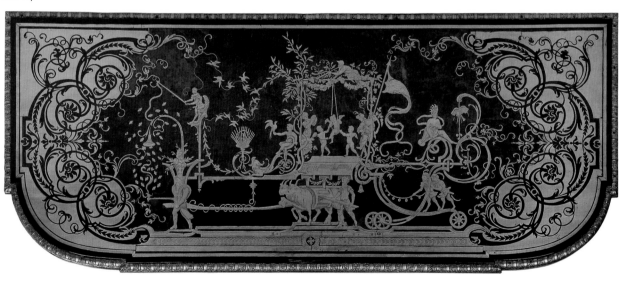

Figure 23
Side table *c.*1705, attributed
to André-Charles Boulle,
veneered with a marquetry
of brass and turtle-shell
and mounted with finely
chased and gilded bronze
mounts.
THE WALLACE COLLECTION,
INV. F424

Figure 24
Marquetry table top
attributed to André-
Charles Boulle, *c.*1705.
THE WALLACE COLLECTION

that, for the sake of the integrity of the design, most cabinet-makers wished to
do just this. Within his Louvre workshop protected by royal patronage, Boulle
was able to design, cast and finish his own mounts. There is no doubt that Boulle
was extremely accomplished in this, and that for some of his designs he made
effective use of the talent of other major sculptors of the time. This was the
period when, rather than being used simply for functional purposes such as
protecting the corners or providing handles or hinges, bronze mounts took on a
purely decorative dimension. As Boulle's bronze mounts were made in the same
workshop, his furniture designs are exceptionally coherent in terms of both the
marquetry and the mounts which are designed to work together. One of the
best examples of this is the wardrobe attributed to Boulle and dating from
around 1700 (THE WALLACE COLLECTION, INV. F61). On the left door, Boulle has
represented a famous episode taken from Ovid's *Metamorphoses*. Sculptural gilded
bronze mounts depict Daphne fleeing from Apollo while the reclining figure
of her father, Peneus, helps her to escape by transforming her into a laurel tree.
While the transformation of her hands and head is represented principally in
bronze, the laurel branches continue into the background marquetry. When
Boulle uses foliate scrolling as a decorative feature in his marquetry, bronze
mounts again underline and follow the same pattern. Thus a variety of factors –
his talent for design and his virtuoso ability as a craftsman, but also his solid
experience of traditional techniques and the opportunity of producing an entire
piece of furniture in one single workshop – were responsible for elevating
Boulle's art to a level that few of his followers would ever attain.

Side table, by A-C Boulle, c.1705 (fig.23)
An example of Boulle's work in the already well-established medium of metal
and turtle-shell marquetry is this side table, probably derived from one made
in 1701 for the royal menagerie. The Chateau de la Ménagerie at Versailles was
an elegantly furnished octagonal pavilion surrounded by enclosures for exotic
animals. The six legs and frame of the table-top are veneered in *contre-partie*
Boulle marquetry of turtle-shell inset into a background of brass, whilst the
centre of the table top is veneered in *première-partie* Boulle marquetry of
engraved brass set into a turtle-shell background. The turtle-shell of the
background has deteriorated over time, giving it its current slightly patchy
appearance.

   The symbiotic relationship of the bronze mounts and the marquetry is
particularly marked: note the way the crescent-shaped satyrs' masks are designed
to fit into the upper concave curves of four of the table legs, or how the foliate
tendrils of marquetry flow out from the central female mask. The design of the
table-top is a fanciful caprice. This type of light-hearted decoration, known as
singeries or *grotesques,* was particularly fashionable at the time. The source for
the decoration of this table is a sixteenth-century engraving by Cornelis Bos.

Figure 25
This *commode* was made
by Antoine-Robert
Gaudreaus in 1739 for the
bedchamber of Louis XV
at Versailles. A simple
geometrical parquetry in
purple kingwood and rich
red *satiné* is used to set off
the richly chased and
gilded bronze mounts of
Jacques Caffiéri.
THE WALLACE COLLECTION,
INV. F86

The central motif of the marquetry top (fig. 24), is an extravagant carriage on which a monkey driver is whipping a swarm of bees. Under a central canopy of branches and floral swags, cherubs dance, make music and play with Cupid, who is seated on a swing. A satyr on top of the canopy blows a trumpet while a flight of birds eddies around the main figures. Two oxen and a human driver plod silently along, bearing the weight of the carriage and forming a strong base for the whole composition. A man in a feathered head-dress plays on a hurdy-gurdy at the rear of the procession while two more monkeys plot mischief below him. Flowers, birds, swags and scrolls add to the light whimsical character of the marquetry. The success of the design relies as much on the blank areas of turtle-shell and brass as on the decorated parts. There is a large expanse of plain turtle-shell around the figurative design, which is compensated by areas of plain brass at the edges of the table top. Between these two zones lies a complex pattern of strap-work, foliate scrolls and stylised floral forms. The table is stamped with the name of the cabinet-maker René Dubois (1737-98) who certainly repaired the piece and who was probably responsible for the addition of the *cassolette,* or small vase-shaped brazier, situated underneath the table on the centre of the stretcher. Boulle himself did not stamp his work.

It was not only Boulle who responded to the fashion for metal marquetry. Many of his contemporaries, such as the younger cabinet-maker Bernard I Van Risen Burgh (*c.*1660-1738), by whom there are a desk and a clock in the Wallace Collection (INV. F59 and F40), were active in this medium. The Wallace Collection also owns a nineteenth-century desk (fig. 45) which is a faithful copy, commissioned by the 4th Marquess of Hertford, of the bureau of the Elector of Bavaria, the original being now in the Louvre.

FIG 25

In 1715 André-Charles Boulle officially handed over his workshop to his sons but it is probable that he never stopped working. The fire in 1720 in his workshop had a serious effect on his production, as did the near bankruptcy Boulle suffered, brought about by his passion for collecting old master drawings and prints, and by the desperate state of the royal coffers from the 1690s onwards. Some of his later works, including the wardrobe with a clock dating from 1715 in the Wallace Collection (INV. F429), have been criticised by some scholars who have argued that Boulle became out-dated and was unable to respond to the changes in fashion that took place towards the end of his life. When Boulle died in 1732, at the age of eighty-nine, the little that remained of his workshop was divided between his sons. Two of them continued to work in the Louvre until their own deaths, producing heavily derivative work based on their father's designs, but which failed to attain the brilliance of his productions.

Régence style furniture

Louis XIV died in 1715 and was succeeded by his great-grandson. The new king was only five years old and a regency was established under his uncle, Philippe duc d'Orléans. The political change was matched by changing styles of living and interior decoration. Floral marquetry furniture and Boulle marquetry declined in popularity, being slowly replaced by the simpler geometrical veneered decoration called parquetry. Fashion in the 1720s dictated opulent forms of furniture with strict and regular parquetry decoration contrasting with elaborate, heavy bronze mounts. The Wallace Collection's commode (fig. 25) by Antoine-Robert Gaudreaus, (c.1682-1746), which was delivered in April 1739 for the new bedchamber of Louis XV at Versailles, is one of the most celebrated and representative objects from this period. The complicated *bombé*-shaped commode is simply veneered, with geometrical parquetry made of kingwood and *satiné*, but mounted with extraordinarily complex gilded bronze mounts by the renowned *fondeur-ciseleur* (caster and chaser of bronze mounts) Jacques Caffiéri (1678-1755). The main decorative feature is unquestionably these bronze mounts, for which the veneering acts as a restrained background. It should be remembered, however, that the balance of the piece has been adversely affected by time, since the bronze mounts have not aged in colour and texture as obviously as the wood, which has become discoloured. When delivered, the kingwood would have been a bold, dark purple colour, which would have contrasted dramatically with the rich red of the *satiné*.

By the time of Boulle's death, marquetry had become practically a lost art. The bronze mounts which had, during Boulle's lifetime, taken on such importance in the architecture of furniture, became the dominant feature of French furniture in the following decades.

THE 1740S AND
THE REVIVAL OF MARQUETRY

The concept of the domestic interior underwent radical reassessment during the eighteenth century. Furniture design moved away from the functional to encompass style, comfort and luxury. Furniture fabrication not only involved the cabinet-maker but was a multi-guild process. The eighteenth century was the age of bronze mounts, but the exorbitant cost of making them could not be absorbed speculatively by the cabinet-maker, who therefore had to rely on firm orders from wealthy customers. The guilds of bronze-founders, chasers and gilders were fiercely protective of their rights with respect to those cabinet-makers who attempted illegally to cast their own bronze mounts. Only a few cabinet-makers in the history of French furniture-making succeeded in evading these rules, usually for reasons such as royal patronage. The most notorious example of the breaking of guild regulations is the case of Charles Cressent (1685-1768), a cabinet-maker and sculptor who on no fewer than three occasions, in 1722, 1733 and 1743, was brought before the guilds of bronze-makers to answer charges that he had made his own bronze mounts, and was repeatedly ordered to use the specialist bronze master-craftsmen instead. In the second half of the eighteenth century, bronze mounts cost up to half of the total resale value of a piece of furniture. The financial problems this presented for craftsmen making furniture resulted in a new way of designing and selling furniture through the intermediary of the *marchands-merciers*. The rise of this guild of *marchands de tout, faiseurs de rien* (merchants of everything, makers of nothing), as coined by Diderot and d'Alembert, would be the most important factor in the design and production of furniture in the second half of the eighteenth century. ❧

Figure 26
Detail of the side of the filing cabinet by Jean-Pierre Latz, decorated with a marquetry of mostly formalised flowers set against a *satiné* background.
THE WALLACE COLLECTION

Figure 27
Filing cabinet by J-P Latz,
*c.*1750.
THE WALLACE COLLECTION,
INV. F82

The marchands-merciers

Ordinary furniture was still made and sold by cabinet-makers but the most intricate, expensive and highly fashionable pieces were mainly designed and sold by these *marchands-merciers,* who would commission work from members of the different guilds involved. *Marchands-merciers* were responsible for the introduction of many new fashions into France, including the use of Japanese lacquer-work panels, which were cut out of imported Japanese coffers or screens and then incorporated into French-designed furniture. A few years later the *marchands-merciers* would develop the novel idea of fitting decorated porcelain plaques onto furniture. Both the panels of Japanese lacquer and the porcelain plaques were highly prized, so they were bought and supplied to the cabinet-maker by the *marchand-mercier,* who would then in turn take the completed piece of furniture. Of course, a few cabinet-makers tried to become *marchands* as well as makers, but with limited success. As individual creativity in the cabinet-makers was not encouraged by the *marchands-merciers*, who sought to control and direct taste, very few cabinet-makers managed to attach their name to a recognisable design or style, and these, such as Oeben and Riesener, all worked to some extent under the patronage of the king.

The perennial preoccupation of French eighteenth-century cabinet-makers was money. Throughout the century, France experienced repeated and severe economic crises. As bronze mounts were so expensive, even the most important cabinet-makers were forced to some extent into the undecorated market, despite the fact that the profit margins were lower. It is possible to find in the sale rooms today plain-veneered pieces by Oeben and Riesener as well as the more ornate examples like those in the Wallace Collection. Paris was by far the largest centre producing luxury goods, with huge numbers of artisans employed. The guild system for the division of labour was financially burdensome since the cabinet-maker, who usually managed each project himself, always owed money to his sub-contractors. A creative cabinet-maker who was economically successful to the end of his working life was very rare.

The revival of marquetry in the 1740s is therefore not attributable to cabinet-makers, as they lacked the resources to launch new fashions, but to one of the most creative and fashionable *marchands-merciers* of the time. Thomas-Joachim Hébert (1713-1774) enjoyed particular success in Paris during the period 1737 to 1750 and may already have been responsible for the idea of using Japanese lacquer-work on French furniture. In 1745 he delivered to the royal family, for the first time in many years, pieces of furniture decorated with floral marquetry. The titular Cabinet-maker of the Crown (*ébéniste de la Couronne*) at that time was Antoine-Robert Gaudreaus but the royal family seems to have preferred the taste of the designer/decorator Hébert, who was then using the cabinet-makers Bernard II Van Risen Burgh (called B.V. R.B, *c.*1696-1766) and Mathieu Criaerd (*c.*1689-1776).

The revival of floral marquetry

The revival of floral marquetry was a slow process, with early floral marquetry of the 1740s, for example that created by B.V.R.B, being composed of formalised flowers rather than the naturalistic flowers favoured by Boulle. Rococo taste, which reached its height during the reign of Louis XV, (reigned 1715-1774) demanded curvaceous *bombé* forms which lent themselves to sinuous, flowing patterns of decoration. By the 1740s the grand, masculine pieces of furniture were generally being replaced by more delicate, feminine pieces suitable for the smaller *appartements* of the period. The small occasional table became fashionable in France as late as the 1740s. Typical marquetry work produced in France during the 1740s involved the inlay of formalised flowers, cut from the natural end-grain of a piece of kingwood, into a background of tulipwood, creating a strong contrast of purple flowers against a reddish background. The flowers were arranged in such a way that they formed a pattern of foliate scrolling rather than simulating an arrangement of real flowers. At the same time a more even balance between bronze mounts and marquetry began to be seen. Most cabinet-makers and designers of furniture had, by 1740, returned to employing bronze mounts to set off, rather than dominate, the veneered surface.

Jean-Pierre Latz (*c.*1691-1754)

Parisian cabinet-makers soon responded to the fashion for floral marquetry. Flowers appeared in the decorative arts as rococo taste took hold. One cabinet-maker who played a role in this revival was Jean-Pierre Latz, first recorded working in Paris in 1719. Already well-known for his Boulle marquetry veneered clock cases, Latz, like B.V.R.B, experimented with end-grain kingwood floral marquetry. At first the flowers were simply formalised rosette shapes, but these were succeeded by more finely-designed floral marquetry motifs towards the end of his life. More Parisian makers

followed the new fashion and it was not long before flower-mania was revived and taken to new heights. Indeed, in 1733 there was even a new outbreak of bulb speculation, this time in hyacinths.

Filing cabinet or Serre-papiers,
by Jean-Pierre Latz, c.1750 (figs.26 and 27)
The sides of this filing cabinet perfectly represent the period of transition in Latz's work, with their mix of formalised and more realistic floral decoration. The general form of the piece, with its exaggerated curvaceous *bombé* shape and the complex asymmetrical gilt-bronze mounts is highly rococo. While the flowers are becoming more realistic, they are still formalised and do not seek to depict any botanically identifiable species. Most of the flowers are made of end-grain kingwood, crudely designed and inlaid into a background of quartered *satiné*. Some flowers are however slightly more realistic in design whilst others have been stained in an attempt to introduce colour.

Latz's more realistic flowers were a precursor of a major episode in the history of French marquetry. The craze throughout Paris for floral marquetry and the quality of execution subsequently achieved would mark the period from the late 1750s up to the 1780s as the high point of marquetry in France.

FIG 27

5　JEAN-FRANÇOIS OEBEN AND THE
HIGH POINT OF FRENCH MARQUETRY

Jean-François Oeben (1721-1763)

In his short life Jean-François Oeben would propel French marquetry
to the status of an art form, equalled only by Boulle before him. He
was born in 1721 near Aix-la-Chapelle, now Aachen in Germany. In the
Germanic principalities the taste for and production of floral marquetry
had been continuous since the sixteenth century. Little is known of
Oeben's early life but it is assumed that he trained under a Flemish
master before moving to Paris sometime before 1749. He set himself
up to live and work in the Parisian centre for cabinet-making, the rue
du Faubourg Saint Antoine, to the east of the Bastille. This street had
attracted cabinet-makers since the Middle Ages because the abbey of
Saint Antoine offered ancient privileges of protection against the strict
guild regulations. Oeben's origins may have helped him to settle in
Paris among some of the most influential cabinet-makers of the time,
including the German immigrant Latz with whom it is possible that
the newly-arrived Oeben worked. He was therefore in touch with the
latest developments in fashion from the start. Between 1751 and 1754
he rented a mezzanine from the last surviving son of Boulle, Charles-
Joseph Boulle, who was still operating his father's workshop in the
Louvre. This was Oeben's first workshop in a royal building, an
environment which undoubtedly had a great influence on the young
craftsman. In 1752, Oeben delivered to Lazare-Duvaux some frames
decorated with floral marquetry. Lazare-Duvaux (*c.*1703-1758) succeeded
Hébert as one of the most influential *marchands-merciers* in France and
was a favourite supplier to the royal court and, in particular, to
Louis XV's *maîtresse-en-titre,* Madame de Pompadour. ✍

Figure 28
Madame de Pompadour,
seen in this portrait by
Drouais completed in 1764,
was mistress to Louis XV
and a powerful patron of
the arts. The table in the
foreground, of colourful
green burr veneer, has
been attributed to Oeben.
Paintings like this provide
evidence of how furniture
may have appeared in its
original condition.
© NATIONAL GALLERY,
LONDON

From this time onward, Oeben's position and prestige seem to have grown enormously and when in 1754 Charles-Joseph Boulle died and Oeben could no longer stay in the Louvre workshop, he was granted a workshop in the royal *Manufacture des Gobelins* where he would stay until 1761. In 1761, he became a master in the cabinet-maker's guild and moved to another workshop in the Arsenal, as the Gobelins workshop had become too small. The Arsenal, where weapons were made as well as stored, contained many metal workshops, so this new location allowed Oeben to have his own locksmith's forge. The Gobelins workshop was left under the control of Oeben's brother, Simon.

There are many points of comparison between Oeben and André-Charles Boulle. As well as being excellent cabinet-makers and *marqueteurs*, they shared the same passion for metalwork. Both masters are known to have personally involved themselves in the metalworking processes, but unlike Boulle, Oeben's interest lay not so much in bronze but in iron and steel. Oeben's pieces of mechanical furniture, incorporating intricate mechanical devices, have great charm both because of the secret compartments often hidden within the structures and of the automatic opening mechanisms, which he made one of his specialities. In 1760, Oeben made a wheelchair for the nine year old duc de Bourgogne, the elder brother of the future Louis XVI, who was suffering from a progressive disease of the bones and the lymphatic glands, of which he was to die within the next year. The mechanical ingenuity and the master-blacksmithing ability displayed in the wheelchair, which could be manoeuvred and adjusted in height, and was fitted with trays for reading and eating, was greatly admired by Oeben's contemporaries.

Between the early 1750s and the end of his life in 1763, Oeben was responsible for producing a wide range of furniture, often with complicated mechanical devices. By the 1750s, although still predominantly rococo in style, the curves of the furniture he made had evolved into less exaggerated and more restrained lines. The now gracious sweeping forms needed only the addition of a few bronze mounts to emphasise their elegant appearance. The surface decoration had become, once again, the main feature and the quality of the piece was in accordance with the refinement and complexity of the marquetry. During the thirteen years of Oeben's Parisian career, his marquetry style developed from formalised rosette shapes, reminiscent of Latz, to highly naturalistic tied bouquets of flowers and elaborate basket arrangements. Like Boulle, Oeben's later flowers are perfect in their detail and are botanically identifiable. It is very likely that the marquetry style developed by André-Charles Boulle was closely followed by his son and that, during the years 1751 to 1754 when he was working in close proximity, Oeben was influenced by Boulle's style. In addition to his accomplishments as a *marqueteur* representing the world of nature through the medium of wood, Oeben also further developed the art of parquetry, inspired perhaps by the highly fashionable Japanese lacquer-work. He created many new

Figure 29
Combined toilet and
writing table, produced in
the workshop of Oeben,
c.1763-64 (fig.30).
THE WALLACE COLLECTION

repeating geometrical patterns which were taken up by his followers of the next generation. Oeben's pieces are now relatively rare, but they have always been appreciated by collectors for their finesse and their quality of execution.

Toilet and writing-table (table de toilette), workshop of Oeben, c.1763-64 (figs 29 and 30)
This lady's toilet and writing-table bears the incised mark of Jean-François Leleu (1729-1807). The table, however, is almost certainly a product of the workshop of Oeben where Leleu was trained and worked until 1763. Recent conservation of this piece has revealed a sophistication of construction and attention to detail characteristic of the work of a mature cabinet-maker such as Oeben himself. One of the finest pieces of furniture in the Wallace Collection, the table displays many of the best qualities associated with Jean-François Oeben's work. The complexity of the mechanical devices argues for an attribution to Oeben of, at least, the design of the table. The locking devices appear to have been custom-made in the Oeben workshop and are not of the type used by Leleu in his stamped work. The marquetry belongs to the recognised style of Oeben and bears striking similarities to designs firmly attributed to him. Additionally the Leleu mark differs in form and spelling from the usual, recognised stamp of Leleu adopted when he set up his own workshop in 1764. Whilst it is possible that Leleu executed this piece, Oeben may, as master of the workshop, also have been involved in its design and even aspects of its production. Oeben did not

FIG 29

Figure 30

Combined toilet and
writing table *c.*1763-64,
typical of the finest works
produced in the workshop
of Oeben. Ingenious
mechanical devices,
geometrical parquetry
and fine floral marquetry
demonstrate a level of
talent matched by only a
few cabinet-makers.
THE WALLACE COLLECTION,
INV. FIIO

stamp much of his work and, as their styles are similar, it is always difficult to
separate the work of Oeben from that of his two famous apprentices, Leleu and
Riesener.

The small table serves the combined purposes of a toilet table and a writing
desk. It has an elegant and unassuming exterior, but, once opened, reveals
extremely skilful mechanical work and an exquisite interior. Unfortunately it is
not known for which wealthy client this outstanding piece was made. A single
lock opens all four drawers and allows the top to slide back. The two side
drawers are fully extendable and each contains a lidded box which, once the
drawers are fully open, can be pulled forward to surround the user, seated in
front of the table, and allow her easier access to the contents of the drawers.
When the top is slid back a panel, located on top of the upper front drawer, can
be pulled forward for use as a writing surface. When this lid is in turn pulled
forward the user gains access to silvered metal ink wells and a pen compartment
beneath. For use as a toilet table the lid is hinged back to reveal, on its underside,
a mirror. Another lid when opened exposes the interior of the upper front
drawer, with space for cosmetics and other toilet articles. The table's design
reflects the transitional period between the rococo and the neo-classical, the
slight curve of the leg harking back to the end of the rococo while the straighter
lines, geometrical parquetry and bronze bay-wreath garlands anticipate the neo-
classical. The bronze mounts may have been modelled by J.-C.-T. Duplessis *fils*
(*c.*1730-1783), a celebrated goldsmith and sculptor who worked in the tradition
of his more famous father; they too are reminiscent of the rococo in their
curving, naturalistic forms, particularly the handles. The ram's heads marking
each corner, characteristic of the type of mounts used in Oeben's workshop, are
finely modelled and chased. The mounts, balanced in size and form so as not to
distract from the veneered surface decoration, work perfectly within the context
of this piece.

All four sides are decorated in parquetry, using two different patterns. Most
of the space is veneered in a design of overlapping circles, a common Oeben
design, which in origin can possibly be traced back to Japanese lacquer-work of
the seventeenth century. The simulated cube design, inspired by Roman mosaic
work, which appears in the centre of the front and back, is a geometrical pattern
again often found in Oeben's work. The device of a *trompe l'oeil* perspective
pattern of infinite cubes was used by Oeben to decorate entire pieces of
furniture, as well as in conjunction with other forms of decoration. The
parquetry sides of the cubes are made of a pink/red tulipwood while the tops
of each side are of grey-stained sycamore. This original colouring of mixed pinks
and greys is again very rococo in style. Unfortunately the colouring is now
somewhat altered with age and probably less striking than when it was new. The
parquetry is framed by a continuous border of cross-banding similar to that on
the table-top.

The marquetry composition on the top of the table (fig. 59) represents a basket of flowers, a motive often found in decorative arts of the rococo period. The basket is minutely rendered with precise shading giving volume to the cane-work. The flowers are naturalistically depicted and individually identifiable. The basket itself contains large peonies, while sprays of double roses, narcissi, Spanish jasmine, daffodils and wall-flowers are arranged around the central basket. Two styles of flower decoration may be seen in the composition: the peonies, or roses, in the basket are more generalised and have the dark centre characteristic of Oeben's earlier work; the outer flowers are more naturalistic and derive from engravings by Tessier. The degree of detail is truly admirable: the rose twig is modelled complete with its thorns, while the leaves have jagged edges and are shaded along the central vein to give a three-dimensional effect. Delicate rose buds complement the flowers, which are made of different woods, some stained and some natural. The peonies to the far left and right of the basket are made of bright yellow berberis, while the narcissi are made of pearwood, which may originally have been stained but has now reverted to its original pinkish-white colour. While the form of the flowers is perfect in every detail, the colours applied to them were often not so realistic. The *marqueteur,* as here, often used black and white engravings as his sources for flower designs. It may be that, working in Paris, he had little exposure to real natural examples of the flowers he was depicting. Using as wide a palette of colours as possible allowed the *marqueteur* to widen the perceived range of flowers, providing additional variety within the composition. The leaves and stalks are all executed in dark stained woods which, in Oeben's time, would have varied in shade. Some of the dark wood approximates to browner shades, which may have been preferred by the maker as they contrast better than green against the grey background. The design comprises a huge number of individual pieces and it is the number of the cutting lines that give the flowers and other parts of the composition their definition. Once cut and shaded in hot sand, these individual pieces were precisely inlaid into a background of grey-dyed sycamore to give a seamless picture using the advanced inlay technique. Despite the very ordered look of the basket of flowers, two narcissi at top centre break slightly into the border strip. This again seems to be a characteristic motif in the work of Oeben and gives the impression that exuberant nature cannot always be contained.

The floral composition is set within a complicated frame of interlaced cross-banding. This triple cross-banded tulipwood pattern weaves around itself and forms repetitive loops and Greek key patterns. It has a symmetrical appearance which is, in fact, slightly asymmetrical. This frame is in turn set into quartered tulipwood veneer. The grains of the tulipwood of the background and the cross-banding alternate in direction so that, although made of the same wood, the cross-banding stands out from the background. The edges of the cross-bandings are finely inlaid with a black-stained and a white holly border strip.

Copy of the roll-top desk of Louis XV:
the original by Oeben and Riesener, the copy by Dreschler, 1855-60 (fig.31)
In 1760 Oeben was given the most important commission of his career; the
design and fabrication of a roll-top desk for Louis XV, for his study at Versailles.
The roll-top desk or *secrétaire à cylindre* was a recently-created design, which
can be securely attributed to the mechanical talent of Oeben. The finished
object, the original of which is at Versailles, is a masterpiece of cabinet-making,
marquetry, metalwork and mechanical ingenuity. The completed desk was so
admired that in 1786 Louis XVI commissioned a similar writing-table, without
the roll top, from the cabinet-maker then in his service, Guillaume Benneman
(d. 1811). This table, which was intended to be placed next to the original desk
at Versailles, is now part of the Rothschild collection at Waddesdon Manor
(National Trust). The 4th Marquess of Hertford, father of Sir Richard Wallace,
recognised the significance of the roll-top desk and commissioned a copy from
the cabinet-maker Dreschler, which was made between 1855 and 1860. This copy
is now on display in the Wallace Collection. Even though the piece is only a
reproduction, the splendour and grandeur of the original are evident. This piece,
probably the first copy ever made of the desk, marked the beginning of a long
history of further copies made for appreciative collectors who would never be
able to acquire the original. Indeed, the wish to possess this magnificent regal
desk is still as strong today as it was in the nineteenth century, and copies have
been made in France as recently as 1994.

The original desk is signed by Jean-Henri Riesener (1734-1806) and was
traditionally attributed to him. Twentieth-century scholars of furniture history
have reassessed the contribution of Oeben and now credit him with part of the
work. When work started on the desk in 1760, Riesener was only an employee
in the workshop of Oeben. Although Riesener was undoubtedly enormously
talented, as his later works were to demonstrate, the design and basic conception
of the desk must have originated with Oeben. As well as Riesener, we know that
a Flemish cabinet-maker/*marqueteur,* Wynant Stylen also worked on the desk
under Oeben's supervision. When Oeben suddenly died in 1763, Riesener took
over the direction of the workshop on behalf of Oeben's widow, finishing a
number of pieces in the process of construction. The extent of Oeben's
contribution can be determined by studying the inventory of his workshop
compiled after his death. The inventory tells us that scale models had been
made, that the carcase was mostly completed, that the marquetry was in
progress and that the bronze mounts were modelled, cast and in the process of
being finished. In 1769, the finished roll-top desk was delivered to Louis XV with
the name of Riesener inscribed in the marquetry. Riesener's *mémoire* (or record
of sale) for the desk shows that he had difficulties in the adjustment of the
mechanical devices and clock, and that the marquetry and bronze mounts were
completed under his supervision.

Figure 31
This roll-top desk is a faithful copy of the one started by Oeben in 1760 and finished by Riesener in 1769 for Louis XV's study at Versailles. Lord Hertford commissioned this copy from the cabinet-maker Dreschler in the 1850s.
THE WALLACE COLLECTION, INV. F460

This desk inspired much admiration at the time of its completion and delivery, perhaps surprisingly given that by 1769 its *bombé,* rococo lines had already passed out of fashion.

Riesener's bill to the King came to 62,985 *livres,* around £1.85m. in today's money, making the desk probably the most expensive piece of furniture ever made. The marquetry made up a substantial portion of the price, representing around one-sixth of the total value, or one-third of the value of the cabinet-maker's work, the metal work, including bronze mounts, accounting for at least half the value.

FIG 31

Figure 32
The complexity and variety of the marquetry decoration on this roll-top desk, signed by Jean-Henri Riesener and dated 1769, make it one of the finest examples of marquetry furniture in the Wallace Collection. INV. F102

Roll-top desk made for the comte d'Orsay, by Oeben and Riesener, c.1770 (fig.32)
This major piece of furniture in the Wallace Collection is closely related to the Versailles roll-top desk for Louis XV. The desk, a simplified version of that of Versailles, is stamped and signed by Riesener. Some furniture scholars have argued that this desk may have been a forerunner of the Versailles desk and that the conception and design of it should likewise be attributed to Oeben. The comte d'Orsay was the son of a wealthy financier and tax-collector. Before purchasing the desk he had been a captain of dragoons, which accounts for the

FIG 32

military trophies that decorate the sides. Louis XV created him comte d'Orsay in August 1770, the year of his first marriage. The grandeur and magnificence of this piece, delivered around the same time, are striking, with the lion masks and feet suggesting the power and fortitude of the desk's first owner. Although dating from the beginning of the neo-classical period, the *bombé* shape of the desk and the naturalistic bronze mounts look back to the rococo. The desk is unmistakably masculine and formidable, the size, the bronze mounts and the marquetry all contributing to the impressive effect.

The desk is decorated in two distinct styles of marquetry, floral and pictorial. Floral marquetry is found on the lower front and back and on the left and right panels of the flat top. This type of marquetry is distinctively Oebenesque. For example, careful study of the marquetry of the drawers at the front right reveals a bouquet of flowers loosely tied with a fat satin bow, the design extending over the two drawers without interruption. Although edges of the marquetry disappear under the handles the composition, with its central bow, is obviously designed to accommodate these handles. Four distinct species of flower may be found in the marquetry on this drawer and, like the toilet and writing table (fig. 30), they are mainly derived from Tessier engravings which were extensively used in the workshops of Oeben and Riesener. The identifiable flowers include daffodils and carnations, naturalistically portrayed and finely cut. The fluidity and freedom of the floral composition is in keeping with the rococo characteristics of the piece. A similar tied bouquet, comprising different flowers including a tulip, decorates the two front left drawers, and the central front panels are also of delicate floral marquetry. The tips of the leaves in these central panels overlap the border in the same manner as the narcissi on the toilet and writing table (fig. 30).

The floral marquetry compositions are echoed on the lower back section of the desk. Here the larger bouquets are positioned so that they spring in towards the centre of the desk, with their ribbons located towards the edges of the compositions. The flowers are larger than on the front and the design is uninterrupted by handles. The design on the back left-hand panel (fig. 8), with its lilies also derives from Tessier engravings. The sides and the entire top half of the desk are covered in a different type of marquetry. Here the panels are pictorial rather than decoratively floral, with only the flat top having floral marquetry. These larger designs are more consistent with the heavy masculinity of the desk. The roll-top is decorated with three marquetry panels, of which the centre one shows the attributes of Poetry consisting of a lyre, an inkpot with quill and three books, surrounded by three roses and a laurel branch. The entire composition rests on a pattern of simulated marble, repeated in panels on the upper half of the desk. The left-hand circular panel, framed by a wreath of laurel leaves, shows a dove with a letter in its beak, possibly a reference to the comte d'Orsay's marriage in 1770. The matching right-hand circular panel shows a Gallic cock.

On the back of the desk are panels representing Geometry and Astronomy, with terrestrial and celestial globes, referring to the skills necessary for successful navigation: the reading of charts and the reading of the stars. Between these panels in the centre of the upper back of the desk is a female figure in profile, holding a figure to her lips and personifying Silence. The upper sides of the desk have marquetry representations of military trophies, including cannons, shot and grenades, drums, a sword and a flag. The lower panels each contain the monogram ORS, for Orsay (fig.33), surrounded by emblems representing the fruits of the earth and the fruits of the sea, emerging from cornucopiae.

Figure 33
Detail of the monogram on the roll-top desk for the comte d'Orsay (fig.32).
THE WALLACE COLLECTION

FIG 33

6

RIESENER, LELEU
AND THE LEGACY OF OEBEN

The next twenty years would see the production of marquetry of almost unsurpassable quality. By the time of Oeben's death, floral marquetry had attained an unrivalled sophistication, with craftsmen and *marqueteurs* starting to fully understand and exploit the potential offered by marquetry techniques. Cabinet-makers of this generation profited from the fact that marquetry was now a common skill in furniture-making, so the experience gained by earlier generations raised the overall standards of workmanship. The skilled *marqueteur* could represent almost any subject he chose with such facility that the final result appeared to be truly a 'painting in wood'. From the 1760s onwards, landscapes with ruins, trophies of music, artists' tools and militaria, as well as images and portraits of people, become common subjects in marquetry. After three hundred years during which inlay techniques had been refined and developed, the designs chosen for marquetry during the late eighteenth century had ironically become very close in spirit to those seen in the Renaissance Gubbio *studiolo*.

Two of the cabinet-makers who can be credited with the greatest contributions to the continuity and development of the art of marquetry were trained in the workshop of Oeben. Jean-François Leleu and Jean-Henri Riesener may both be considered to have extended the work and the influence of Oeben beyond his early death. ❧

Figure 34
Detail of the side marquetry from the *secretaire à abattant* by Leleu (fig.35).
THE WALLACE COLLECTION

Figure 35

Despite the predominantly neo-classical style of this secretaire *c.*1772-74 by Jean-François Leleu, the influence of the master Oeben is still apparent, particularly in the floral marquetry doors which are of remarkable quality containing a large variety of exotic and dyed woods.

THE WALLACE COLLECTION, INV. F301

Jean-François Leleu (1729-1807)

Leleu, slightly the elder of the two, would probably have joined Oeben's workshop before Riesener. The usual age to begin an apprenticeship was between twelve and fourteen. Leleu was one of the few really successful cabinet-makers of his time to have had native French origins. He not only achieved the respect of his cabinet-making colleagues, through his work for the Guild of Cabinet-Makers, but he also had the rare good fortune whether through chance

FIG 35

or through business acumen, not to end his life as a bankrupt. When Oeben died in 1763, Leleu was thirty-four. Oeben's widow was allowed by the King to continue her husband's cabinet-making business and Leleu may have hoped to be asked to take on the management of the workshop, a position obtained instead by Riesener. There is certainly strong evidence of Leleu's animosity towards Riesener, seen for example in Riesener's documented complaint against Leleu to the Paris police. Shortly after his departure from Oeben's workshop, Leleu, together with one of his workmen, was accused of attacking Riesener in the street. Nevertheless, having quitted Oeben's establishment, it seems that Leleu had no difficulties, financial or otherwise, in opening his own. As early as 1764 he was able to become a master and he soon began to enjoy considerable success amongst the aristocracy. The 8th prince de Condé, Louis Joseph de Bourbon (1736-1818), became a major customer of Leleu and commissioned many pieces from him for the refurbishment of the Palais-Bourbon (now the National Assembly). Leleu's early works were much influenced by Oeben whose later works anticipated neo-classicism. The neo-classical style became fashionable in the 1760s, following the re-discovery of the ruins of Pompeii (where excavations began in 1748) and of Herculaneum (excavations from 1738). At the same time the rococo, which remained the preferred style of Louis XV, maintained its popularity.

The pieces of furniture delivered between 1772 and 1774 to the prince de Condé are to some extent examples of the new neo-classical style. Pieces from the collection of the prince, one of the first aristocrats to escape revolutionary France in 1789, are today to be found in some of the world's finest art collections.

Secrétaire à abattant, by Leleu, c.1772 (fig.35)
The most important piece of furniture by Leleu in the Wallace Collection is the *secrétaire à abattant,* possibly made for the prince de Condé's Palais-Bourbon refurbished between 1772 and 1774. This secretaire has not suffered from modification and is essentially in its original condition, despite damage from light as well as the wear and tear of two hundred years. The overall look of the piece is very masculine, with a strong architectural form emphasised by the columnar effect of the sides and other architectural decoration. The secretaire is square and sculptural in form, geometrically organised and displays many features associated with the neo-classical movement. These include the fluted corners surmounted with bronze mounts of acanthus leaves and with female masks wearing crowns of bay leaves, lion-feet supporting the secretaire, scrolling decoration and acanthus leaf mouldings. There is an exuberance in the use of lavish gilt-bronze mounts and the extravagant decoration. It is somewhat incongruous that the main surface decoration, amongst all these neo-classical motifs, comprises three framed marquetry panels reflecting strongly the influence of Oeben.

opposite page

Figure 36
The inside of the
secretaire by Leleu,
*c.*1772 (fig.35), having been
preserved from the light,
has retained its bright
colours. Tulipwood is
framed with stringings
of white and black holly
set into a border of
purpleheart.
THE WALLACE COLLECTION

The marquetry of the drop front comprises instruments for music,
astronomy and geometry placed around an urn draped with laurel leaves and
displayed on a marble ledge. A ribbon, supporting a garland of flowers, frames
the centre trophy. The marquetry of the two lower doors comprises classical
baskets of flowers, which are suspended by ribbons from *trompe l'oeil* nails.
The compositions of the two doors appear symmetrical but are in fact slightly
different. All three marquetries are inlaid into a background of grey-stained
sycamore designed to simulate the effect of light falling on grey silk and are
surrounded by a border of purpleheart. This type of floral arrangement is
reminiscent of Oeben and would not have been particularly fashionable in 1772.
As with Oeben's own floral marquetry, it is possible to identify botanically
virtually every flower used in the composition. The delicacy of the flowers
overflowing the suspended baskets and the intricate foliate tendrils winding
their way around the ribbons, attest to lessons well-learnt in Oeben's workshop.
The quality of the execution is superb. Woods used in the marquetry include
holly, stained sycamore (of many colours, including black), purpleheart,
pearwood, tulipwood and whitebeam. The darkening of the marquetry
background and the fading of the designs make the composition more difficult
to read, so that it is harder for us today to appreciate fully the role the marquetry
would have played in the piece's overall appearance. Recent conservation has
revealed a variety of stained greens in the flower leaves. They show how carefully
the *marqueteur* chose his colours, varying them according to whether he was
depicting one end or the other of a branch, or a newer or an older leaf. Unlike
the seventeenth-century *marqueteur,* who made use of mostly natural highly-
coloured woods, exploiting the wide range of new imported species, the late
eighteenth-century *marqueteur* seems, as here, to have preferred dyeing clear
European woods to achieve his desired palette.

The repetitive marquetry design employed on the sides of this secretaire is
a favourite decorative device of Leleu. Indeed, a similar secretaire in the Musée
des Arts Décoratifs in Paris is entirely veneered with this type of marquetry.
A small writing-table by Leleu in the Wallace Collection (INV. F323) is also
veneered primarily with repetitive marquetry and parquetry.

The quality of the bronze mounts is exquisite. The careful chasing of the
details of the faces of the masks, of the acanthus leaves, and of the mouldings
catch the light to the best effect. The mounts are typical of this period in the
way in which they obscure the real function of the secretaire. In the lower part,
the existence of two doors is hidden by a single bronze moulding, encircling both
doors, which is discreetly cut in the middle to allow the doors to open. It seems
that furniture designers of the time were preoccupied with disguising the real
function and construction of a piece of furniture, in favour of emphasising the
unity and grandeur of its external appearance.

The magnificence of the outward appearance of this piece is matched by the

quality of its construction. The use of counter-weights makes the opening of the heavy drop-front so smooth that one finger is sufficient to control its movement. The interior of the secretaire is designed to cater for everything the owner might need for his correspondence: an adjustable reading table, with fittings for pens, ink and drying-powder, as well as many drawers and compartments (fig. 36). There is also a secret compartment which, at the push of a button, springs up to reveal four tiny drawers. The name secretaire derives from the fashion for secret compartments, which were commonly built into this type of furniture.

The secretaire is made from the best quality materials. Every iron and steel lock is covered with a purely decorative gilt-brass plate. The drawers are made from solid *satiné*, rather than the usual oak, despite the high cost of this South American imported wood. The red colour of the *satiné* of the inside of the drawers still survives, as this part has been protected from sunlight. The colours of the interior drawer fronts, veneered with tulipwood contrasting with purpleheart, are so vibrant that it is difficult to imagine that once the outside too would have looked equally bright. The fronts of the drawers are shaped to give an element of fluidity to the design. The interior of the lower part includes two drawers and a safe compartment which requires a third key to allow the safe to slide forward and the lid to be opened.

It seems that Leleu never sacrificed quality for increased productivity, unlike his rival Riesener. Following his work for the prince de Condé, Leleu would make furniture in accordance with the changing fashions. In 1780, he took on his son-in-law as an associate, and in 1792 handed over his business to him. Leleu was elected a principal (*juré* or assessor) of the Guild of Cabinet-Makers and indeed his own work followed the best principles of the Guild – traditional furniture of the finest quality, which however made no real attempt to push forward the frontiers of design and manufacturing techniques.

Pierre-Antoine Foullet (*c*.1732-*c*.1780)

Pierre-Antoine Foullet was the son of the cabinet-maker Antoine Foullet (*c*.1710-1775) who specialised in making cases for mantel and long-case clocks, particularly in Boulle marquetry. Foullet was not one of the great cabinet-makers, despite occasional important commissions such as the pair of corner cupboards now in the Wallace Collection (INV. F273-4), delivered to Versailles by Gilles Joubert (1689-1775) in 1773 for the comte d'Artois (the future Charles X, who would reign 1824-30) and probably made by Foullet. Financially Foullet's career was disastrous. His work is often characteristic of the transition period, a good example being the secretaire in the Wallace Collection (fig. 37) made *c*.1777, which demonstrates strong neo-classical influence, while lacking a mature understanding of the style and retaining some rococo features.

Figure 37
This secretaire, signed in the marquetry by Foullet, was made *c.*1777. Of an extremely fashionable neo-classical design with Roman landscape and ruins, the rich decoration of the piece is however not entirely successful.
THE WALLACE COLLECTION, INV. F299

Secrétaire à abattant, by Foullet, c.1777 (fig.37)

This secretaire is one of a group of three by Foullet, identical in design and grandeur. The strong classical flavour of the piece is seen in its general architectural decoration and classical decorative elements. The combination of marquetry design and bronze mounts on the drop-front is highly classical in spirit, whilst a depiction of classical ruins is used as a background for the imposing gilt-bronze trophy decoration made up of bay leaves, a lion's head and Roman-style armour below a coat of arms. The sources of the marquetry composition can be traced to a series of engravings published in 1776-77. An odd touch is the charming dragon-fly appearing top-right. This secretaire could be regarded as over-decorated, and in quality of execution it does not compare to work by Oeben, Leleu or Riesener. The Roman landscape is shown against a sky of blue-stained sycamore (now turned green with age) and includes a ruined portico, a colonnade and an obelisk. A landscape is a very difficult subject for a *marqueteur* and was not often attempted, even by the great cabinet-makers of this period. Whilst the *marqueteur* responsible for this piece obviously had a good understanding of the technical side of marquetry, the drawing lacks depth and cohesion, although it must be acknowledged that the discoloured state of the wood makes the composition more difficult to appreciate.

The lower doors each have an inset oval panel of marquetry surrounded by a gilt-bronze frame of ribbon and bay leaves. These oval marquetries portray, on the left, military arms and, on the right, scientific equipment. A floral basket is set beneath the two oval frames and a swag of flowers drapes itself around the strap-work banding. The basket is flat and superficial compared with similar baskets by Oeben, Leleu and Riesener. The decoration of the sides includes marquetry designs of columns and flowers. The floral marquetry is also less distinguished than that of the other three masters. Foullet's flowers, while intended to be naturalistic, lack the finesse and precision of Oeben. There is not the range of flowers found in the work of Oeben, Leleu and Riesener and Foullet's flowers are more difficult to identify.

Jean-Henri Riesener (1734-1806)

During the nineteenth century Jean-Henri Riesener was considered to be one of the three greatest names in French cabinet-making, along with Boulle and Cressent. Twentieth-century research has added further names to this list but Riesener should still be considered one of the most influential and important cabinet-makers of the eighteenth century.

Riesener was an immigrant craftsman who moved to Paris around 1754, from his birthplace of Gladbeck, a town east of Cologne near the Rhine. Oeben had come from the neighbouring province, a fact which almost certainly helped Riesener, at the age of twenty, find a place in Oeben's workshop. The young Riesener was ambitious and his career made a spectacular early advance with the unexpected opportunity of succeeding Oeben in 1763. The early works finished and signed by Riesener, despite being conceived and begun by his former master, placed him at the forefront of French cabinet-making. Even though Madame de Pompadour, a major patron of Oeben's workshop, died in 1764, followed ten years later by Louis XV, for whom Riesener completed the roll-top desk, the latter seems to have been favoured by the new king, Louis XVI (reigned 1774-1792). He was also popular with the young queen, Marie-Antoinette (1755-1793), herself a passionate collector. Riesener continued working within the protected environment of the royal Arsenal, but seems to have maintained good relations with the Guild of Cabinet-Makers, paying his subscriptions and being received as a master in 1768. When after 1763 he started to operate the workshop on behalf of Oeben's widow, he was obliged to use the name and the stamp of his deceased master. Becoming a master in his own right allowed him to stamp furniture with his own stamp. In 1774 the Cabinet-maker to the Crown, Gilles Joubert (1689-1775), who was then eighty-five years old, made an agreement with Riesener to sell him this privileged sinecure. From that time, Riesener had full access to the *Garde Meuble de la Couronne* and, over a period of about ten years, he made more money from supplying the King than any other cabinet-maker. From 1774 to 1784, he was paid the enormous sum of 938,000 French *livres*, which should be seen in the context of an average salary of six hundred *livres* a year for a skilled Parisian gilder or cabinet-maker.

The Wallace Collection possesses one of the finest collections anywhere of furniture by Riesener, including many objects with a royal provenance. The collection includes furniture from throughout Riesener's career, beginning in the 1760s with pieces begun by Oeben, and continuing into the 1780s and the end of his most productive phase. Three important secretaires from the Collection illustrate the changing fashions in marquetry during Riesener's career; the earliest one is representative of the high-point of marquetry while the latest, from 1783, illustrates its demise.

Secrétaire à abattant, by Riesener, 1780 (fig.38)

The first secretaire was delivered to Versailles in 1780 for the *cabinet intérieur* (or private study) of Marie-Antoinette. It is part of a group of seven secretaires of a similar design. At least two of these are stamped Oeben rather than Riesener, implying that they were made before 1768, and some scholars believe that this model may even have been designed by Oeben. The Wallace Collection secretaire is the latest in date and was delivered in 1780, about fifteen years after the creation of the earliest known version. By the time of its delivery, despite its grandeur and richness of decoration, the Wallace Collection secretaire was, in style and design, distinctly out of fashion. It is not surprising that after only three years in Marie-Antoinette's *cabinet intérieur,* it was sent to store and was replaced by another secretaire also today in the Wallace Collection (fig.40).

In 1785 the first secretaire seems to have been moved out of store to the small royal residence of Saint-Cloud for use by Louis XVI. It would stay in Saint-Cloud until it was sold after the Revolution in 1794-95. The somewhat masculine appearance of this secretaire, with the two bronze heads and the male masks, also seems a strange choice for Marie-Antoinette, although, with her love of secret devices, she would certainly have appreciated the strong and ingenious locking system. The secretaire is, however, a masterpiece in terms of the quality of its marquetry. The marquetry on the sides depicts sprays of delicate flowers, set into separate enclosed lozenges, and would have been more appropriate to Marie-Antoinette's taste, as would the two beautiful floral compositions on the lower doors. Most of the flowers on this secretaire can be found on pieces dating from Oeben's lifetime, but their arrangement, particularly with the use of two classical urns and the strict maintenance of the compositions within the clearly delineated borders, makes concessions towards the new taste for the neo-classical. The lozenge pattern on the sides is inspired by Japanese lacquer, this particular design appearing to have originated with Riesener. The current condition of the drop-front marquetry does not do justice to Riesener's skills as a *marqueteur*: it requires careful observation to appreciate the complexity of the design of the triumphant Gallic cock standing on a trophy comprising a flag, a snake, a hand mirror, a telescope and a caduceus (two snakes entwined around a rod: the symbol for peace). The innumerable separately-cut pieces, elaborately shaded, would have given this marquetry a quality evoking painting. The secretaire was conserved during the 1940s and the long-term results of the techniques then used were not well understood. Whilst the procedures adopted were consistent with common restoration practice of this date, the products then applied on top of the marquetry have deteriorated with the result that the subtleties of the design are now obscured by unsightly brown, striated marks. Nowadays, conservation techniques and products are carefully tested before use and treatment of this secretaire should form part of the conservation programme in 2002.

Secrétaire à abattant, by Riesener, 1783 (fig.40)
The secretaire which replaced the 1780 piece in Marie-Antoinette's *cabinet intérieur* at Versailles is veneered entirely in thuya burr. This was a clear presage of the new style which signalled the end of marquetry, a style which could be termed the French mahogany period. The thuya burr secretaire was delivered in 1783, together with a matching corner cupboard also in the Wallace Collection (INV. F275) and a chest of drawers. The richness and the naturally decorative nature of the brightly coloured reddish-brown burr would have created an effect which virtually simulated marquetry. The wood was used simply for its intrinsically beautiful and decorative qualities, although it appears that the burr effect was heightened by the insertion of tiny wooden dowels into the veneer.

FIG 38

FIG 39

Figures 38, 39 and 40
These secretaires, made by Riesener for Marie-Antoinette, were all delivered to Versailles between 1780 and 1783. THE WALLACE COLLECTION, INV. F300 (FIG 38); INV. F302 (FIG 39); INV. F303 (FIG 40)

The bronze mounts play a major decorative role in the design of the object and are feminine in style. Flowers, which on the earlier secretaire were featured as subjects for marquetry, appear here in the form of minute three-dimensional arrangements and sprays within the bronze mounts. The central oval bronze plaque depicts a Sacrifice to Love and the rectangular plaque in the frieze, Mercury with two naked children. Decorating furniture with representations of chubby infants had now become more appropriate given Marie-Antionette's status as a mother, particularly after the birth of the Dauphin in 1782. In their delicacy and complexity, and in their application as simple moulding frames for each panel of thuya burr, the bronze mounts achieve an unprecedented degree of refinement.

Secrétaire à abattant, by Riesener, 1783 (fig.39)
In the same year, 1783, another secretaire of very similar architectural design was delivered for Marie-Antoinette, this time to the Petit Trianon at Versailles. In form, it shares the same basic design as the other secretaires. It is veneered in a grille-like marquetry pattern which approximates to parquetry but is actually a fret-work design encompassing many lozenges, each of which contains a stylised

Figure 41
This marquetry panel,
made in the advanced
inlay technique using
innumerable originally
highly-coloured pieces,
is a good example of
David Roentgen's work
in the 1780s.
COURTESY OF THE
TRUSTEES OF THE
VICTORIA AND ALBERT
MUSEUM

water-lily. The use of this grille-pattern does not mark an advance in design or fashion, unlike the radical use of thuya burr veneer on the other secretaire. Indeed this type of grille-pattern marquetry, which again may derive from Japanese lacquer-work, can be found on many pieces of furniture by Riesener from the early 1780s. The fashion for floral marquetry has moved on, to be replaced by a taste for more repetitive motifs. This decoration still has its source in the work of Oeben, but it has been taken to a completely new level by Riesener. When delivered it would have been considerably more colourful: the grille pattern in rich purpleheart would have contrasted strongly with the white holly of the backgrounds into which were inlaid water-lilies with pinky-brown pearwood petals and centres of bright yellow berberis. The bronze mounts are similar to those of the thuya burr secretaire but are more complex and elaborately floral. Riesener also supplied a chest of drawers in the same style for the *cabinet intérieur* in December 1780. This too is now in the Wallace Collection (INV. F247).

By 1780 the outrageously curving rococo and the heavily masculine, early neo-classical styles had both been superseded by a new age of elegance, which may be regarded as the culmination of two hundred years of furniture design. It is extraordinary that only three years separate the floral marquetry and masculine appearance of the first secretaire from the refined elegance of the latter two. By the late 1770s fashion and taste in furniture had moved away from the styles which Riesener had learned from his master Oeben, and which he had employed so successfully since Oeben's death. In the entire history of French furniture, in which the king's name is commonly used to denote a particular style, the significance of the death of one king and the crowning of his successor was never greater than after the death of Louis XV in 1774. The change in taste was made even more dramatic because of the interests of a new queen, whose acquisitive passion for fashion and art was far more forceful than that of the monarch.

Riesener's success with the new style of plain veneered furniture would be very short-lived. After having made an estimated seven hundred pieces of furniture for the royal family during the ten years between 1774 and 1784, Riesener lost the privilege of supplying the King. The financial crisis in France, which was one of the principal causes of the French Revolution, had a major impact on the Court consumption of luxury items. Most cabinet-makers dependent on royal orders would be bankrupt by 1789. In 1784, Thierry de Ville d'Avray became the new *intendant général des Meubles de la Couronne,* an administrator of the royal furniture collection, replacing Pierre-Elisabeth de Fontanieu, whose family had been responsible for the administration of the *Garde Meuble* since the time of Louis XIV. This turned out to be disastrous for Riesener. Thierry took the opportunity not only to reorganise the Court system of furniture procurement but also to economise, and Riesener was expensive. His impressive volume of supply to the French Court had only been made

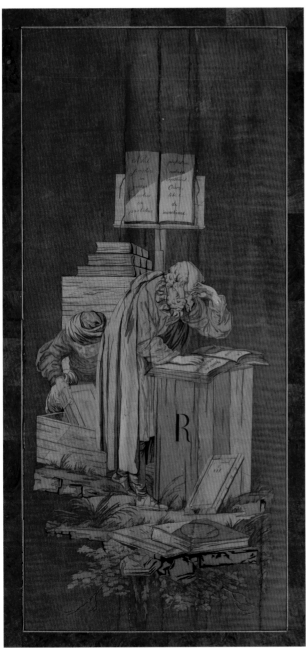

FIG 41

possible by sub-contracting much of the work to other independent cabinet-makers in Paris. These cabinet-makers supplied Riesener with parts (carcases, metal-work) and sometimes with the entire piece of furniture. In 1786 it was noted by the administration of the *Garde Meuble* that the quality of furniture supplied was declining and yet the prices asked by Riesener were considerably higher than those of his competitors, and indeed his suppliers. After an unprecedented ten years of success, Riesener would be the first cabinet-maker of the eighteenth century to lose the King's favour. The *Garde Meuble* decided to commission furniture using the sculptor Jean Hauré *(entrepreneur des Meubles de la Couronne)* as the co-ordinator of each major order or to order direct from a *marchand-mercier*. Riesener's position was made even more insecure by the fact that, despite the increased refinement of his production by the mid 1770s, he was not making the most fashionable furniture available in Paris. Effectively Riesener reached around 1784 a peak of accomplishment, beyond which he was unable to progress. There were other more exciting cabinet-makers from whom the King and Queen could commission their furniture, including Adam Weisweiler (1744-1820) and David Roentgen (1743-1807) who supplanted Riesener in the King's favour in the mid 1780s. The Wallace Collection does not own any examples of furniture by Roentgen, although examples may be seen in the Victoria & Albert Museum (fig. 41). His marquetry was of extraordinary quality and his ability to represent a convincing scene in wood was of a standard unachieved by anyone before or since. His marquetry typically represents figurative classical, *Chinoiserie* and theatrical scenes, birds and floral compositions. These scenes are comprised of an extraordinary number of individually-cut pieces in various highly-coloured stained woods, which make Roentgen's work the closest approximation of that of any *marqueteur* to paintings in wood.

7   Decline and Revival:
The Story from the 1780s

In the early 1760s Oeben made for Madame de Pompadour the first French pieces of furniture veneered entirely in mahogany. Although this wood had been used extensively in England for several years, the French traditionally preferred complex and intricate marquetry decoration. Oeben can ironically be credited with conceiving the style of the future which would mark the end of marquetry, the medium in which he himself had excelled. Oeben and his patron, however, both died too early to play a significant part in advancing the fashion for mahogany along the path it was destined to take. It was towards the end of the 1780s that plain veneers indicated the clear direction of furniture fashion for at least the next thirty-five years. ಌ

Figure 42
Detail of *sécretaire à abattant* attributed to Molitor, *c.*1790. By this time plain mahogany veneer was prized for its intrinsic beauty.
THE WALLACE COLLECTION, INV. F309

Figure 43
This *commode* was originally veneered with a marquetry of Bourbon *fleurs-de-lys*. The marquetry was removed sometime between 1793 and 1807, to be replaced with a plain mahogany veneer.
THE WALLACE COLLECTION, INV. F246

New craftsmen in favour with the King, including Benneman, Weisweiler, as well as Riesener, were all producing plain mahogany-veneered furniture during the 1780s. There was no place for marquetry in this austere style, the quality of the piece instead relying on the choice of wood with an interesting grain. The Wallace Collection has many examples of pieces from this era, including a roll-top desk by Riesener of *c.*1785 (INV. F277) which is veneered in the most wonderful mahogany and is elegantly framed by restrained gilt-bronze mounts. Another example, attributed to Molitor (d.1833) is a *secrétaire à abattant, c.*1790 (fig. 42) which makes use of the best mahogany and employs bronze mount decoration in the most sophisticated fashion.

In addition to the economic recession which lasted from 1774 to 1792, the French Revolution, not surprisingly, had a disastrous effect on those cabinet-making workshops which specialised in the luxury end of the market. Most of the cabinet makers, including Benneman and Roentgen, went bankrupt, although strangely Weisweiler did not. With the execution of the royal family and the elimination, either by execution or emigration, of the old aristocracy, the important cabinet-makers lost their main customers and only a few remained in

FIG 43

favour with the new revolutionary government. Most royal furniture did, however, survive the worst violence of the Revolution and, rather than being destroyed, much of it was offered for public sale between 1793 and 1795.

Whilst the selection of furniture for sale did not observe the logic that, with hindsight, the modern French state might have liked to have seen applied, some conscious thought was given already at this time towards preserving the nation's history, some of the finest furniture being retained for the newly-created *Muséum Central des Arts*. Some of the more ordinary furniture was also kept by the French State for use by the new government. Many of the pieces were sold for a fraction of what they had cost when they were made, only a few years earlier. Riesener himself bought back, for a small sum, some of his own furniture, in the expectation that the monarchy would be restored and he would be able to sell it back at a profit. Unfortunately for Riesener, subsequent financial difficulties obliged him to sell these pieces again soon afterwards, with no financial benefit to himself.

Although the Revolution therefore did not by and large result in the destruction of furniture, hatred for Louis XVI, his aristocracy and his government, resulted in deliberate damage to many marquetry pieces. Much furniture of the *ancien régime* was veneered in marquetry which symbolically extolled the Bourbon dynasty. Even the pieces which were preserved for the museum had to have these royalist tributes removed. Riesener himself was asked to remove and replace, with an ordinary trophy, the original central marquetry on the cylinder of the roll-top desk of Louis XV, which had been finished in 1768 and which depicted the traditional attributes of the monarchy. The double interlaced Ls on each side of the roll-top desk were also removed, to be replaced by two porcelain plaques imitating Wedgwood.

In some cases the marquetry was replaced by marquetry of equal quality, but in many other cases it underwent more dramatic change. The commode made by Leleu in 1772 for the prince de Condé (fig. 43) would originally have been veneered with exquisite marquetry of similar quality to that still to be seen on the secretaire by Leleu (fig. 35). However, at some date between 1793 and 1807, the entire piece was re-veneered in mahogany. This dramatic transformation was probably not simply prompted by the wish to eliminate the *fleurs-de-lys* marquetry decoration, but also by the new taste for plain veneers. In the same way, another commode made originally by Riesener in about 1782 (THE WALLACE COLLECTION, INV. F248), of the same model as the two commodes delivered to Marie-Antoinette at Marly, lost its marquetry in favour of a simple mahogany veneer.

The combination of the French Revolution's insistence on the removal of royal symbols and the prevailing fashion for mahogany furniture resulted in the permanent destruction of some of the finest marquetry decoration created during the eighteenth century. The change of taste was also responsible for the temporary downgrading of the status of the French *marqueteur* in favour once again of that of the maker of bronze mounts.

The nineteenth century and the revival of eighteenth-century styles

In 1794, the Reign of Terror was brought to an end with the execution of the Jacobin leaders. After the unpredictability of five violent years of revolution, the period from 1794 to 1799, called the Directoire, established a new calmer social order. With the stabilising of government, money once again became available for art and luxury items. For those cabinet-makers who had survived the lean revolutionary years, the Directoire was a period of re-birth. The Revolution had not entirely by-passed the furniture industry. In 1795, a new system of weights and measures, called *metric,* was made mandatory, although the evidence suggests that many cabinet-makers ignored this directive. More significantly, the powerful guilds which had governed French trades since the Middle Ages were dissolved by a law passed in 1791 *(Loi Le Chapellier).* New ways of designing and manufacturing furniture were permitted, with for example cabinet-makers being granted the liberty to control all stages of the manufacturing process, from the carcase to the bronze mounts. These reforms offered some entrepreneurs the opportunity to create furniture manufacturing industries, one of the most noteworthy examples being that of the Jacob family. Originally a family of chair makers, the workshop of the two Jacob brothers developed to such an extent that, by 1803, it employed more than three hundred workers. Jacob *frères* was the favourite furniture manufacturer of Napoléon and his first wife, Joséphine de Beauharnais. The small workshop of the eighteenth century was threatened with disappearance forever.

The French state was still proud of its achievements in the arts and encouraged the development of art and craft industries, including furniture. From 1801 to 1806, outstanding works of art were displayed to the public in exhibitions of the products of industry *(des produits de l'industrie).* French craftsmen, trained by and often still working in the tradition of eighteenth-century craftsmen, could produce furniture of extremely high quality. Mahogany furniture, without the contribution of marquetry, remained fashionable for many years, in spite of the Continental Blockade from 1806 which prevented, amongst other things, the importation of mahogany into France. However, Napoléon's attempts to steer fashion in favour of French products were notoriously ineffective; even Joséphine could not be persuaded to wear Lyons silk once English muslin gowns had become all the rage. It seems that when it came to the latest styles, ways to circumvent the blockade were always to be found and in fact the Empire style made the taste for mahogany-veneered furniture more dominant than ever. The British blockade did ultimately affect the available stocks of mahogany, so that indigenous woods began to be used instead. By the late 1820s paler woods such as sycamore, ash, ash burr and satinwood had become popular.

A significant change in fashion began to be seen in the mid 1820s. Charles X's daughter-in-law, the young duchesse de Berry, was particularly interested in the

opposite page

Figure 44
This *première-partie* Boulle marquetry coffer on stand in brass and turtle-shell was originally catalogued as Louis XIV but has recently been re-dated to *c.*1820 when good quality copies of eighteenth-century furniture were fashionable.
THE WALLACE COLLECTION, INV. F47

arts. As Charles X came to the throne as a widower, the duchesse de Berry to some extent occupied the role normally taken by the sovereign's consort, and aristocratic society followed her lead. Marquetry reappeared in the simple form of small detailed foliate decorations, but very much as an accent rather than a main design feature.

Louis-Philippe, less aristocratic and more approachable than his distant Bourbon cousins, came to the throne after the short revolution in July 1830 at the head of a new constitutional monarchy. The new French royal family, and indeed those elsewhere in Europe, although to a lesser degree, modified its taste to accord better with that of the new rising middle classes. Although, personally, Louis-Philippe had little interest in furniture, he did demonstrate a preference for Boulle marquetry furniture, the fashion for which had recently been revived. The new social order, although unquestionably materialistic, did not ape the eighteenth-century elite by spending such enormous sums on furnishings and decoration but still had a certain amount of disposable income. Perhaps ironically, given the political upheavals, from the 1840s onwards cabinet-makers were making furniture in the eighteenth-century style and, by the 1850s, the rococo-revival style had become predominant. It seems that there existed a nostalgic wish to evoke the perceived stability of the past by focusing on more traditional styles. In 1852 Napoléon III proclaimed himself Emperor of the French and embarked on a project of rebuilding France, choosing neo-rococo as his official style for architecture and decoration. This was part of a deliberate policy designed to bolster his new regime, by conspicuously reminding Frenchmen of their country's former greatness in the arts. Napoléon III's consort, the Empress Eugénie, was fascinated by the *ancien régime* and by Marie-Antoinette. She not only created interiors in the Louis XV and Louis XVI styles, but also endeavoured to restore to the royal residences eighteenth-century pieces not sold by the revolutionaries. Of course, the nineteenth century had to out-do its predecessor, so the eighteenth-century styles were improved upon, becoming more highly decorative, more flamboyant and, to our eyes, more gaudy. It was not uncommon practice to 'improve' older pieces by adding extra embellishments so that they would compare with newly made fashionable furniture. The new fashion was, therefore, merely an invocation of the old rococo with little inherent creativity, but it did mean that marquetry entered upon another period of glory during which the craft flourished, with work of an extremely high standard being produced. At the 1851 Great Exhibition in London, French manufacturers carried off many of the major awards for furniture and marquetry. The understanding and knowledge of marquetry had not been lost, despite nearly fifty years of limited demand.

The Industrial Revolution, developing from the mid-eighteenth century, transformed many production techniques. Marquetry techniques were among those that evolved to accommodate mass-production and to meet the increased

Figure 45

A copy of the celebrated
writing-table made for
the Elector of Bavaria
*c.*1715. The copy was
commissioned by Lord
Hertford from the London
upholsterer, cabinet-maker
and dealer John Webb,
following the exhibition
of the original desk in 1853.
It is a faithful reproduction
of the desk as it appeared
in 1853, including several
gilt bronze mounts added
in the nineteenth century
and subsequently removed.
The quality of the
marquetry shows the high
level of craftsmanship in
the nineteenth century.
THE WALLACE COLLECTION,
INV. F461

demand from the *nouveaux riches*. The nineteenth century was therefore a
period of high demand, to which cabinet-makers responded with a huge volume
of production, ranging from furniture of the very highest quality to cheap
mass-produced pieces.

The 4th Marquess of Hertford was a collector who recognised the nostalgic
and historic value of old pieces of furniture. Hertford purchased many original
eighteenth-century pieces which had come onto the art market after the
Revolutionary sales and he also sought to augment his collection by
commissioning copies of the greatest furniture of the past century, such as the
famous roll-top desk of Louis XV. Most of the copies in the Wallace Collection
date from the 1850s. These copies and imitations were extremely well-made,
using the best materials and respecting the finest craftsman's traditions of the
previous century. Distinguishing nineteenth-century copies from eighteenth-
century originals in the Wallace Collection can be difficult, the marquetry on
these pieces often proving of equal quality to that applied to the original pieces
of furniture. However, from today's perspective it is perhaps regrettable that
these nineteenth-century copies were made to match the original pieces in their
nineteenth-century condition. Since the originals were by then at least sixty
years old, the colours had deteriorated, and any neglect or discoloration was
unthinkingly replicated. Because nineteenth-century copies were made to look
old the marquetry did not seek to employ the range of lavish colours which the
eighteenth-century craftsman had exploited so expertly.

Since the nineteenth-century, marquetry has been primarily thought of as
a characteristically eighteenth-century art-form. It has not played any major
innovative role since then, although it made a small contribution to *art nouveau*
at the turn of the last century and again in the 1920s. There are a few cabinet-
makers today practising marquetry who can still find, using the traditional
techniques, a way of expressing new design concepts. Indeed, certain
contemporary craftsmen have pushed the execution of marquetry to superlative
heights. However, this kind of hand-crafted marquetry is prohibitively expensive
and modern taste seems for the moment to prefer simpler, less decorative forms
of design. It can only be hoped that marquetry will continue to find its place in
people's hearts and lives, enabling this special art to be preserved into future
generations.

FIG 45

8   SOURCES OF MARQUETRY DECORATION

Making marquetry first involves creating a drawing of the chosen subject or taking one from elsewhere. When Jean-Henri Riesener chose to be depicted with a crayon and paper in his portrait by Vestier, now at Versailles, he clearly wished posterity to view him as an artist rather than as a simple craftsman. If we try to define the notion of an artist as someone with original artistic creativity and the craftsman on the other hand as someone who faithfully replicates that artistic creativity, it becomes an interesting exercise to assess into which category eighteenth-century cabinet-makers fall. Whilst we can appreciate easily enough through the quality of the works of art which they created the artistic capabilities of the cabinet-makers of the seventeenth and eighteenth centuries, the amount of truly original content is questionable. Most cabinet-makers, including the greatest names, would have made use at some time of the expertise of an artist or a decorator for the design of the furniture and also for the design and pattern of the marquetry. Direct employment of an artist, however, was rare, being impractical, expensive and only appropriate for the most prestigious commissions. Much late eighteenth-century furniture was conceived by a *marchand-mercier,* who would organise the project and would commission the design and fabrication as required. Some furniture, including much of the grandest was, of course, conceived by the individual cabinet-maker, particularly those makers protected from the guilds by royal patronage. Original drawings attributed to Boulle, for example, still survive today and demonstrate Boulle's own considerable artistic ability. However, this route was financially more risky. ❧

Figure 46
Detail from a lacquer cabinet made in Kyoto for the European market and finished *c.*1680 in Paris (fig.53).
THE WALLACE COLLECTION

Figure 47
Plate 31 from *Le Livre de Principes de Fleurs* engraved by Chevillet, from a drawing by Tessier, has been used as a source for the marquetry of the Riesener work-table (fig.48).
COURTESY OF THE BIBLIOTHÈQUE FORNEY, PARIS

Figure 48
Detail of the marquetry of a work-table attributed to Riesener, *c.*1765-70.
THE WALLACE COLLECTION, INV. F313

Figure 49
Made *c.*1670 for the Trianon de Porcelaine at Versailles, this table, with its marquetry of blue horn and white ivory, was designed to match Louis XIV's collection of blue and white Chinese porcelain. It is one of the earliest examples of European marquetry being directly inspired by the arts of the Far East.
© THE J. PAUL GETTY MUSEUM

FIG 47

FIG 48

The detailed inventories of the Boulle and Oeben workshops describe collections of drawings, paintings and engravings and it is probable that they were not alone among cabinet-makers. It is known that Boulle was a serious collector of and dealer in prints, as well as contemporary and old master paintings, and it seems likely that some of these became the inspiration for, or even the direct sources of, his marquetry. In the eighteenth century, engravings were made in large numbers and were widely distributed, so they were obvious sources for the planning of marquetry decoration. In recent years scholars have discovered the printed sources for many pieces of marquetry from the seventeenth and eighteenth centuries.

The engravings themselves were subject to the vagaries of fashion. The development of international trade and the dynamics of politics, including dynastic alliances, resulted in the spread of currents of taste and culture across Europe and beyond. The seventeenth-century passion for tulips and other flowers led to a taste for floral ornamentation on everything, including paintings and many types of decorative art. Trade with the Far East had an enormous influence, during the seventeenth and eighteenth centuries on every decorative art form, including marquetry. These two examples show that understanding the social and artistic history of a country is as relevant for understanding the sources of decoration as discovering the precise original drawing or print which provided the source for a work of art.

Identifying a precise marquetry source is however often difficult, especially when two or three hundred years have passed since the marquetry was made. The way in which marquetry designs were created makes the task even more difficult. Sources were rarely copied exactly or used in isolation. Very often more than one source was drawn on within any one composition. To appreciate the skill of the *marqueteur* it is necessary to understand, not only his materials and techniques, but also how he reworked his sources in order to create a satisfactory marquetry design.

The influence of Oriental lacquer work

Trade with the Far East intensified during the seventeenth century and, by the eighteenth century, France, together with the rest of Europe, was deeply influenced by the exotic objects arriving from India and China. Japanese items arrived in Europe via the Dutch who were trading with Japan, to the exclusion of other Europeans, from 1639 or earlier. Textiles, porcelain, metal-work and lacquered objects were imported in vast quantities to meet the spiralling demand. Like most of the rich and fashionable elite towards the end of the seventeenth century, Louis XIV collected Chinese blue and white porcelain. The *Trianon de Porcelaine* was created in the early 1670s to display the King's collection of Chinese porcelain, accompanied by furniture by Gole. The furniture was European in form, but incorporated white ivory and blue horn foliate marquetry designed to match the blue and white porcelain on display. A surviving table from this group, now in the Getty Museum (fig. 49), is perhaps the earliest example of European marquetry being influenced directly by the Far East. The long history of oriental influence on marquetry had begun.

Whilst the forms of furniture produced in the Far East were not to European taste nor particularly well-suited for use in Western interiors, the lacquer-work finish was greatly admired. European cabinet-makers did not have sufficient access to the raw product, since the tree which produces the lacquer used by the Chinese and Japanese could not be grown in Europe. As a result, as early as the seventeenth century, European cabinet-makers developed a type of varnish which could be applied to furniture to imitate the high shine of lacquer.

FIG 49

In 1686 Louis XIV received significant gifts from the Siamese embassy which included lacquer screens, cabinets and boxes. During the 1690s, France was engulfed by a Far Eastern mania, which found its outlet in interior furnishing and decorations and even in some of the more outlandish dress-styles of the time. The number of shops in Paris offering for sale oriental objects, including porcelain, textiles, metal-work and lacquer, multiplied. This enthusiasm for lacquer work coincided with the fashion for Boulle marquetry. It soon became evident to cabinet-makers that brass and turtle-shell marquetry could be adapted to imitate the oriental lacquer works. Turtle-shell, which can have a very plastic appearance, has many similar properties to lacquer and the addition of a layer of black pigment behind the turtle-shell increased to a remarkable degree the resemblance between the two types of material. Comparison of lacquer work furniture and Boulle marquetry furniture reveals striking similarities, confirming that cabinet-makers of the time were certainly inspired by Far Eastern lacquer work. Cabinet-makers may well, in an attempt to regain some of the market that they had lost to the fashionable lacquer, have designed their furniture in direct imitation of it. Earlier European attempts to replicate the techniques of Far Eastern lacquer had been scorned by contemporary customers, who regarded them as merely 'pale' copies, and perhaps the stunning success of Boulle marquetry at this time may have been due to it being considered a more successful form of imitation.

FIG 50

FIG 51

FIG 52

FIG 53

Figures 50 & 51

The marquetry above the dial on this clock, attributed to André-Charles Boulle *c.*1720-25, simulates the pattern found on the Kyoto lacquer cabinet.

THE WALLACE COLLECTION, INV. F42

Figures 52 & 53

This lacquer cabinet, made in Kyoto for the European market and finished *c.*1680 in Paris has a motif of interlaced circles which is similar to patterns found on Boulle pieces of furniture. From its earliest appearance in Paris, lacquer work was copied or imitated in marquetry.

THE WALLACE COLLECTION, INV. F18

Although most Far Eastern imported objects were destined for the urban elite and would certainly not have been owned by or been accessible to most cabinet-makers, it is probable that Boulle's position gave him access to the royal collection of lacquer. The Wallace Collection has two lacquer cabinets (fig.53), made in Kyoto for the European market and finished in Paris around 1680. Their sides are decorated with similar landscape scenes, typically Japanese in their simplicity and use of blank space. The fronts have more complicated designs, comprising on each cabinet a landscape depicting houses, water, trees and mountains with figures engaged in different pursuits. The pictorial compositions are framed by a symmetrical and repetitive pattern of interlaced circles, each surrounding a rosette-like flower. The rosette and the interlaced patterns are made of gold and silver powder applied on top of a black lacquer ground. A virtually identical geometrical pattern can be seen, reproduced in Boulle marquetry, on the impressive Four Continents clock (fig.50) by Boulle, made around 1720-25. The area of marquetry above the dial is made from a black turtle-shell background inlaid with interlaced circles and a rosette flower of yellow brass. The striking similarities in colour, brightness and pattern of these three pieces, conceived in countries so far apart, strongly suggest that the Boulle clock design derived from Japanese lacquer work. Similarly, the more simple pattern found on the same clock, below the dial, can be related to the diaper pattern of small roundels, enclosing a foliate lozenge, on a seventeenth-century lacquer box in the Victoria and Albert Museum (fig.55).

Indeed many other geometrical Boulle marquetry patterns of the time can be related to Japanese and Chinese lacquer work, and an oriental influence can be seen in other subjects in Boulle marquetry, such as the pictorial scenes known as *chinoiseries*.

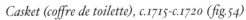

Casket (coffre de toilette), c.1715-c.1720 (fig.54)

This casket, by an unknown French cabinet-maker, is an example of the attempts in France to replicate lacquer-work through the medium of Boulle marquetry. Whilst the design of the casket itself follows European models, its decoration aspires to the exotic. The top and sides are veneered in *première-partie* marquetry of turtle-shell, brass and mother-of-pearl. The pictorial decoration on the other hand derives principally from Chinese sources. The top of the casket shows a hunting scene with two mounted hunters, dogs and a standing figure. At the bottom of the panel is a lake created in mother-of-pearl with two elegant swans. The figures are oriental in dress, as are the trees and the house at the top right. The four side panels show various Chinese figures and oriental landscapes. The composition of the panels and the use of blank spaces derive from Eastern rather than European concepts of design. The *chinoiserie* figures are not entirely understood and there is a primitive quality to the decoration, a consequence of the French craftsman's second-hand knowledge of China and its people. Despite

Figure 54

This small Boulle marquetry casket, made in France *c.*1715-20, is heavily influenced by oriental lacquer work.

THE WALLACE COLLECTION, INV. F34

Figure 55
Detail of a seventeenth-
century Japanese lacquer
box, typical of those made
for the European market.
COURTESY OF THE
TRUSTEES OF THE
VICTORIA AND ALBERT
MUSEUM / PHOTOGRAPHER:
IAN THOMAS

Figure 56
Detail of the inside of the
roll-top desk by Riesener,
made in 1769 for the
comte d'Orsay (fig. 32),
showing the repetitive
marquetry pattern which
Riesener himself referred
to as being in the taste of
Boulle.
THE WALLACE COLLECTION

this clumsiness the casket illustrates well the mania for lacquer at the beginning of the eighteenth century and the success with which brass and turtle-shell could approximate to its appearance.

By the late 1730s a new fashion evolved, whereby original lacquer panels were integrated into the design of European furniture. This practice was led by the *marchands-merciers,* as discussed in Chapter 4. At the same time Europeans refined their techniques for the imitation of lacquer, so that successful simulated lacquers began to appear, such as the *vernis Martin* developed by the Martin brothers. Given this continued fascination with oriental styles, it is not surprising that imported lacquer work was used as a design source for wood marquetry.

Around 1750 cabinet-makers such as Oeben were making furniture with repetitive geometrical patterns similar to those found on Chinese and Japanese lacquer work. A drawing by François Guérin, formerly belonging to Edmond de Rothschild, represents Madame de Pompadour and her daughter Alexandrine (probably made just before Alexandrine's untimely death in 1754 at the age of seven) and shows a mechanical writing table, similar in design to one today in the Louvre attributed to Oeben. The sides of this table are veneered in a repetitive marquetry grille pattern comparable to lacquer work. The toilet and writing

FIG 56

Figure 57
Paintings similar to this
one by Jean-Baptiste
Monnoyer (1636-99) and
his studio were in Boulle's
workshop in 1732. They
were used as the source for
many of Boulle's floral
designs and may also have
been used in Oeben's
workshop.
COURTESY OF SOTHEBY'S
LONDON

table (fig.30) by Oeben, has marquetry of interlaced circles on its sides, which may be a simplified interpretation, without the stylised rosette, of the front border of the two lacquer cabinets (fig.53). It could, however, equally well be based on another lacquer work pattern or could even be a design invented by Oeben himself. As we have seen, Oeben was strongly influenced by Boulle, and it is interesting to ask whether Oeben was in fact imitating the original lacquer works or whether he was recreating Boulle's lacquer-inspired geometrical marquetry. The marquetry pattern decorating the inside of the comte d'Orsay desk (fig.56), by Riesener of *c.*1770, is of the repeating geometrical type. The pattern has striking similarities with those on the Japanese lacquer box in the Victoria and Albert Museum (fig.55), yet being decorated in grey sycamore, deep yellows, purple and white, it would never have approximated to real lacquer. Interestingly, Riesener, when describing the identical marquetry on the roll-top desk of Louis XV, talked of 'mosaic' marquetry in the 'taste of Boulle'. By the second half of the eighteenth century the wood marquetry patterns were made in many colours and had moved away from direct imitation of lacquer. Riesener's interpretation of oriental lacquer therefore rather reflects the long-term current of cultural and artistic interchanges between the Far East and Europe, showing the cabinet-maker responding, both in his choice of design and in his materials, to Parisian fashion which was itself a re-interpretation of the oriental. As the taste for the oriental became more generalised, so interpretations became looser and less dependent on a specific original source.

The use of paintings and engravings as sources of decoration in floral marquetry

The influence of lacquer work was felt by *marqueteurs* throughout most of the greatest periods of marquetry production. As an inspiration, it can only be matched by the role occupied by flowers and certain other natural phenomena, particularly in the floral marquetry of the late seventeenth century and the second half of the eighteenth century. While paintings which can clearly be considered as direct sources for marquetry are rare, the fashion for floral marquetry in the seventeenth and late eighteenth centuries coexisted with the periods when flower painting enjoyed its greatest favour. Floral marquetry originated in Germany and the Low Countries, where there were strong traditions of still-life and floral painting which may have been imbedded in the culture of the immigrant craftsmen working in Paris.

The cabinet-on-stand (fig.21), attributed to Boulle, is the most splendid example of wood marquetry in the Boulle technique in the Wallace Collection. Whilst the cabinet's decoration might well be related to flower paintings of the seventeenth century, it has not proved possible to identify a source, but the fact that Boulle owned a large collection of prints makes it likely that such sources, whether prints or paintings, do exist and will one day be identified.

FIG 57

FIG 58

Figure 58
These plates from *Le
Livre de Principes de Fleurs,*
were used as sources for
the marquetry of the
Oeben table. Many other
floral designs by Oeben,
Riesener and their
contemporaries make
use of these engravings.
COURTESY OF THE
BIBLIOTHÈQUE FORNEY,
PARIS

Figure 59
Marquetry top of the
writing and toilet table
made in the workshop of
Oeben, *c.*1763-64 (fig.30).
THE WALLACE COLLECTION

FIG 59

An unusually detailed document by Jean Hauré concerning the making of a desk, now at Waddesdon Manor, for Louis XVI by Benneman in 1786, reveals how much artists did contribute to the most important projects. At least three different people were involved in the design and production of this particular marquetry. Painted studies for the marquetry were originally made by the artist Girard, while another artist Bertrand drew templates from which the marquetry could be cut and finally, the *marqueteur* Kemp executed the wood marquetry, certainly with the help of other craftsmen. The document also tells us that, while the cost of the marquetry by Kemp was 442 *livres,* Girard was paid 168 *livres* and Bertrand 36 *livres.* Thus the artists' work cost just a little less than half of the value of the *marqueteur*'s work, including the materials, a prohibitive cost in the context of the economics of cabinet-making in eighteenth-century France. It is not surprising therefore that most cabinet-makers who made marquetry in their workshops chose to use prints as the principal sources for their marquetry designs and often used the older and less fashionable prints which would have been less expensive. Few purpose-made drawings for *marqueteurs* were produced and, perhaps not surprisingly, such drawings have not survived.

Although it is difficult for these reasons to identify sources for marquetry, some progress has been made by scholars. In the early 1970s, Sir Geoffrey de Bellaigue was able to establish the link between the later marquetry of Oeben and a book of engravings entitled *Le Livre de Principes de Fleurs* by Chevillet, based on the drawings of Tessier published in the early 1750s by the Widow Chereau in Paris. Study of this book reveals how understandable it is that such prints were popular with the *marqueteur.* The fifty plates fall into two groups, the odd-numbered plates containing floral studies in which simply the outline of the design is traced, whilst in the even-numbered plates the same floral studies are depicted three-dimensionally. The *marqueteur* may well have used the odd-numbered plates for the cutting of his flowers and the even-numbered plates for shading them. Any craftsman, even one with no real talent for drawing, could have made marquetry using this book. The careful superimposition of tracings of eighteenth-century marquetry by Oeben, Riesener and other *marqueteurs* of this period onto the original engravings, conserved in the Bibliothèque Nationale in Paris, has proved conclusively that *marqueteurs* did make marquetry by tracing directly from these engravings. The marquetry top of the toilet and writing table (fig. 59) is a floral basket composition resembling floral basket paintings by artists such as Jean-Baptiste Monnoyer (1636-1699) and his son Antoine Monnoyer (1677-1745). The flowers are of two distinct types, and match those from different stages of Oeben's career. The large flowers in the basket are an early type derived from an unidentified source, whilst the sprays of flowers outside the central basket derive precisely from five different engravings in Tessier's *Le Livre de Principes de Fleurs* (fig. 58) and are typical of Oeben's later work. The plates used are daffodils (Plate 13), narcissi (Plate 15), wall flowers (Plate 27), Spanish jasmine

following pages

Figure 60
Back of a toilet-mirror
attributed to Boulle, *c.*1713.
THE WALLACE COLLECTION,
INV. F50

Figure 61
Engraving after Jean Berain
used as a source for the
marquetry on the back of
the toilet-mirror by Boulle.
THE WALLACE COLLECTION

(Plate 31) and double roses (Plate 43). The prints correspond exactly to the size of the flowers in the marquetry, although there are slight differences between the original engraving and the final marquetry composition for each peripheral spray of flowers. This is a result of the inlay technique and the *marqueteur*'s freedom to 'improve' the composition where he felt this to be appropriate. Not all of Oeben's sources are as easy to identify as this table top. In many cases, whilst the general compositions may be similar, only one flower from a Tessier plate is used and this may often be found within an otherwise completely unrelated floral composition. Because flowers were pre-cut and stored, usually with little regard for their final destination, individual flowers could end up in the middle of an otherwise unrelated floral marquetry composition. The same Spanish jasmine flower found on the bottom left side of the basket on the table top (fig. 59), is also used on many other pieces of furniture by Oeben and Riesener in the Wallace Collection. Often only one or two jasmine flowers appear, and not in the same arrangement. For example, there are two of these jasmine flowers on the side of the Riesener secretaire (fig. 38) and others on the roll-top desk by Riesener (fig. 32).

Trophies and landscapes in wood marquetry

Aristocrats of the *ancien régime* would flaunt their social status by commissioning symbolic trophies in marquetry or bronze, alluding to one's high birth or personal heroism. Knowing the identity and story of the original owner of a piece of furniture can help in interpreting many marquetry decorations. The comte d'Orsay's desk (fig. 32) has trophies of warfare which relate to his career as a captain of dragoons, while the dove portrayed on the roll-top may allude to his forthcoming marriage, which took place shortly after the desk had been made.

The difficulties encountered in identifying the sources of floral marquetry extend, to a lesser extent, to trophies and landscapes. Whilst the *marqueteurs* could make relatively successfully floral compositions out of a 'montage' of many different sources, it seems that *marqueteurs* rarely ventured so far as to compose their own trophies and landscapes. The few sources for trophies and landscapes in marquetry identified so far by furniture scholars show much greater similarities between the engraving and the final marquetry design. As with flower marquetry, however, the techniques used mean that the resulting marquetry will always vary slightly from the original source, often with the removal or addition of certain elements or even with the reversing of the design. Trophies and landscapes are often fairly simple in design, as these two subjects can be difficult to execute successfully in marquetry.

The secretaire by Foullet (fig. 37), made around 1777, illustrates how the *marqueteur* would have made use of engravings available at the time. De Bellaigue's researches revealed that the design of the marquetry on the left-hand side of the drop front was taken from the frontispiece of the fourth book of

Figure 62
Detail of the left side of
the drop-front marquetry
of the Foullet secretaire
(fig. 37) based on an
engraving by Le Canu after
a drawing by Jean-Charles
Delafosse.
THE WALLACE COLLECTION

Figure 63
Frontispiece of *Quatrième
Livre de Trophées contenant
divers attributs pastorals* by
Jean-Charles Delafosse,
engraved by Le Canu and
published *c.*1776-1777.

FIG 62

FIG 63

trophies by Jean-Charles Delafosse, engraved by Le Canu, entitled *Quatrième
Livre de Trophées contenant divers attributs pastorals* and published *c.*1777 (figs. 62
and 63). For this particular piece the original engraving was too small and the
subject too simple to furnish the *marqueteur* with a design for the entire drop-
front, so the marquetry on this piece of furniture is actually a montage including
other, as yet, unidentified engravings. The talent of the *marqueteur*, whether or
not guided by an artist, lay in his ability to arrange within an imaginary landscape
a series of views, in order to create a new one which would satisfy him as an artist
and would also catch the eye of his customers. The Delafosse engravings had
only recently been published when the Foullet secretaire was made. Despite
their expense, the cabinet-maker chose to use these recent engravings in order
to make marquetry in the latest neo-classical style.

One of the reasons why this secretaire is less successful than others in the
Wallace Collection is the disparate range of marquetry sources drawn on within
this one piece. Sources have been identified for other panels. The design for the
oval marquetry in the centre of the two lower doors of this secretaire is lifted,
virtually unchanged, from two soft-ground etchings, taken from the *Premier
Livre de Trophées,* drawn by Alexis Peyrotte and etched by Gilles Demarteau,
published around 1776. The flower marquetry on the lower doors probably comes
from an earlier source, as it was not essential to use expensive contemporary
prints for the more generic floral marquetry.

Sources of decoration of Boulle marquetry

Although the Musée des Arts Decoratifs in Paris houses an important collection of original drawings and designs attributed to Boulle, Boulle is known to have occasionally employed the assistance of an artist or designer and readily adapted available sources of decoration in designing his marquetry. The technique of Boulle marquetry, whilst not lending itself to floral decoration, is suitable for many other types of subjects and in particular foliate scrolling designs. Other scenes, called *singeries,* show monkeys in different postures and activities close to those of humans. The Wallace Collection has based its logo on a *singerie* taken from a Boulle table. Another form, called *grotesque,* depicts grotto scenes of classical gods with attendant monkeys taking the place of classical fauns. The most influential artist of the time, as far as Boulle marquetry is concerned, was the architect and ornamental designer Jean Berain (1637-1711). The son of a gunsmith, he began his career by publishing designs for the decoration of gun-stocks and locks. From 1670 onwards he was employed by the Crown as an engraver and, in 1674, he became the official *Architecte Dessinateur de la Chambre et du Cabinet du Roi.* This post required him to provide designs for royal festivities, ballets, costumes and opera sets. He worked and lodged in the Louvre from 1690 and certainly developed a relationship with Boulle who also worked there. Berain's position as one of the principal artists at the French court led to his designs being widely used by Parisian cabinet-makers and, indeed, Boulle soon started to use Berain's engravings as sources in his marquetry. The toilet mirror attributed to Boulle in the Wallace Collection (fig. 60) is an example of the use of Berain engravings in the design of marquetry. It was supplied in 1713, as part of a Boulle marquetry toilet service, to Marie-Louise-Elisabeth d'Orléans, duchesse de Berry (1695-1719). Berain's engraving has been used in its entirety, with a few small changes. The satyrs adoring Venus in the centre of the engraving have been replaced by two musicians while the two goats at the bottom of the engraving do not appear at all in the marquetry. The marquetry is the outcome of talented interpretation of the Berain engraving, the arrangement of other ornamentation enabling the original engraving to fit neatly into the shape of the mirror back. It is unfortunately impossible to know whether Boulle himself, Berain, or another artist modified the engraving for use on this mirror.

The writing-table in the Wallace Collection (INV. F57) attributed to Oppenordt is another example of the influence which Berain's work had on cabinet-makers of the late seventeenth and early eighteenth centuries. The Boulle-type marquetry top of this writing-table has a central scene taken from an engraving by Marie Daigremont (working 1670-1700) after Jean Berain. The marquetry design copies the engraving virtually unaltered. Indeed, the use of Berain engravings in the making of Boulle marquetry became so common that marquetry compositions of this type were soon called 'Berainesque'.

COLOURS IN MARQUETRY

It is difficult today to appreciate marquetry in a way that would have been possible for an admirer of the art form in the seventeenth or eighteenth century. The ultra-violet rays in sunlight have gravely affected the natural and dyed woods used, leading to discolouration and bleaching. Many of the chemicals used in the dyeing processes were unstable, and exposure to the atmosphere may cause oxidation of the dye or time itself, in the case of fugitive stains, may be sufficient to alter the colours of some of the dyed woods. These problems not only have a detrimental effect on the appearance of the marquetry today but are, unfortunately, irreversible. Other problems caused by factors such as accumulation of dirt or darkening of old finishes can be treated through conservation. ❧

Figure 64
Detail of the satinwood parquetry on the table by Molitor, *c.*1788-90 (fig. 66).
THE WALLACE COLLECTION

FIG 65

FIG 66

Whilst it would be rare indeed to come across a seventeenth or eighteenth-century piece of furniture whose exterior had been, throughout its life, protected from the light, the insides of these pieces can give the modern viewer a better idea of the original colour of the wood. Conservation and security considerations make it impossible for museums generally to display furniture in its open state, but the Wallace Collection periodically organises a small Open Furniture event when selected pieces are displayed in this way for a limited period. Many of the pieces are well worth a second look, including the interior of the Leleu secretaire (fig.36), where the purpleheart, tulipwood veneers and solid *satiné* used inside retain their original vibrant purple, red and gold colours.

Roubo wrote that 'the beauty of the furniture consists in the vivacity of its colours'. The best quality marquetry in the eighteenth century was praised as being 'as good as an oil painting' by a writer in *L'Avant Coureur* of May 1766. Bearing this comment in mind, flower paintings made directly from nature give perhaps some of the best indications of the original colours of floral marquetry. The modern viewer is so accustomed to the natural 'wooden' palette of marquetry today that it becomes difficult for us to accept that real flowers, naturally vibrant and often gaudy, may have determined the original choices of colour for the seventeenth and eighteenth-century *marqueteur*. Although no firm consensus has yet emerged, there is considerable discussion among furniture scholars as to what much marquetry looked like when it was first made. The debate has focused in particular on the most commonly-used marquetry background in the second half of the eighteenth century, dyed sycamore. It is generally agreed that most marquetry compositions from this period use a background of dyed sycamore, which today has taken on a greenish-brown tobacco appearance, where it has been exposed to light. This can be seen for example in the toilet and writing table by Oeben (fig.59) or the

Figure 65

Well preserved original colour can be seen in the woods of the marquetry located inside the Foullet secretaire (fig. 37).

THE WALLACE COLLECTION

Figure 66

This table by Molitor, *c.*1788-90, now faded to a pale brown colour on its exterior, would originally have been as yellow as the satinwood interior which has been protected from light.

THE WALLACE COLLECTION, INV. F321

comte d'Orsay's roll-top desk (fig. 32). Contemporary eighteenth-century evidence, including the popular name of this wood, *gris satiné,* suggests to many scholars that the wood may have been originally dyed grey. However, even where sycamore wood has been protected from the light, the grey has faded, to be replaced by a more green colour. Analysis has revealed traces of the substances which may have been used to dye the wood, and tests aimed at replicating the processes used have indeed produced grey results. It is, however, difficult to prove one way or another and arguments as to whether this sycamore was dyed green or grey will no doubt continue.

Conservation of structurally-damaged furniture can necessitate the removal of marquetry in order to allow the conservator to gain access to the solid wood carcase for repairs. This process carries a potential risk to the marquetry and must be performed carefully, but it can be of enormous interest to the furniture historian. The glued side of the marquetry, which has never been exposed to the light, is revealed, and in many cases the stunning original colours have been preserved. In the case of a roll-top-desk by Riesener decorated with floral marquetry in the Royal Collection (figs. 68 and 69), it became necessary to remove part of the marquetry from one of the sides. Bright pink, yellow and white flowers were revealed, as well as one in a vibrant blue, which was particularly interesting, as it appears green on the exterior of the marquetry. These highly realistic flowers had been inlaid into a greyish background.

The temporary removal of marquetry is regarded as a step of last resort in the conservation process. Sometimes therefore the historian has to rely on other sources or on his own powers of deduction. For example, the sky in the marquetry landscape on the secretaire by Foullet (fig. 37) is now a strange shade of green, although it must be assumed that it started out blue. Tests have demonstrated that eighteenth-century blue dyes subjected to ultra-violet light will turn green. It is, however, impossible for us to understand the exact intensity of the original blue. Home-made dyes of green and blue, whether mixed in the workshop or purchased ready-made from a supplier, would have varied from one batch to another, making it even more difficult for us to be certain about the original colours. In some of the rare examples of well-preserved objects, such as the secretaire by Leleu (fig. 35), more than one shade of green can still be made out in the leaves of the same floral composition. In the painting of 1764 of *Madame de Pompadour* by Drouais, in the National Gallery, London (fig. 28), there is in the right foreground a round work table which can be attributed to Oeben. This table is veneered in a dyed-burr of a intense green colour. It is possible that the painting itself may have been subject to discolouration, or even that Drouais was not accurate in his depiction of this piece of furniture, but it is generally accepted that the painting is accurate and that the table was veneered in some shade of green. Some surviving traces of green dye have been found on eighteenth-century furniture. This colour used in furniture may have been

FIG 67

inspired by contemporary green-glazed porcelain. Porcelain was used extensively on furniture in the eighteenth century, so backgrounds and marquetry of furniture would have been designed to complement any porcelain fittings. The small work-table by Roger Vandercruse, called Lacroix, (RVLC 1728-1799) of *c.*1760 (fig. 67) is mounted with a Sèvres porcelain tray. This predominantly white shallow tray, decorated with a scene depicting foxes and bright-plumaged birds, has a turquoise-blue border, on top of which is overlaid a gilded trellis design with corner cartouches. At mid-height Lacroix has placed a wooden shelf reminiscent in design of the upper porcelain tray. The colours have deteriorated with time but, originally, the centre panel of this shelf would probably have been veneered in pure-white sycamore, with an inlaid design of roses, carnations and jasmine. The outer pattern of the shelf, which now appears green, would have been dyed a turquoise-blue to match the porcelain tray. This green-veneered background is inlaid with a lattice pattern of berberis that would originally have looked as bright as the gilded trellis-work of the porcelain top. As the porcelain has not discoloured, the wood should be imagined as originally possessing very similar colours. The four narrow sides of the table are veneered in an approximately-matching fret-pattern marquetry of pale green stained sycamore, inlaid into a background of purpleheart and dotted, where the trellis crosses, with spots of red wax.

All this evidence goes a long way towards proving that original marquetry of this period was indeed very bright in colour. The easiest way to appreciate the alterations which have occurred over time is through modern reproductions and computer reconstructions. The current exhibition at the Wallace Collection which this book accompanies aims to give the visitor some idea of the real eighteenth-century appearance of marquetry. Modern reproductions and reinterpretations of works by Boulle, Oeben and Riesener can appear shocking when placed next to the now discoloured originals. Over the last decade craftsmen have become increasingly interested in understanding the traditional

FIG 68

Figure 67
The colours of the
marquetry border of the
lower shelf of this work-
table stamped RVLC
*c.*1760, now discoloured
to green and pale brown,
would originally have
replicated the blue and
gold of the porcelain top.
THE WALLACE COLLECTION,
INV. F326

Figure 68
Marquetry detail of
roll-top desk by Riesener,
*c.*1775–80
THE ROYAL COLLECTION
2001, HER MAJESTY QUEEN
ELIZABETH II

Figure 69
This marquetry was
removed from the
Riesener roll-top desk
in the Royal Collection.
The reverse side shows
the original colours of
the marquetry. The blue
flower has discoloured
to green on the exterior
of the marquetry
(photograph shown reversed).
THE ROYAL COLLECTION
2001, HER MAJESTY QUEEN
ELIZABETH II

techniques, which has led to research into many areas of seventeenth and eighteenth-century cabinet-making. Traditional, almost extinct techniques have been recreated, old tools have been examined afresh and old recipes have been re-discovered and tested. This work has also included examination of eighteenth-century recipes for dyeing wood. By carefully selecting wood from the same species used then and by copying recipes from Roubo and others, marquetry has been produced which contains colours which we could not have imagined from the appearance of eighteenth-century furniture today. It must be emphasised however that these modern reproductions are themselves still a personal and subjective interpretation. Many of the recipes are imperfect and require some modification whilst, for example, the amount of time the wood is left in the dye will affect the intensity of the colour. The modern copies may not show the exact original colour but they are certainly useful tools, which give a new perspective on the historical objects.

The discolouration of wood over time was the subject of complaints as early as the eighteenth century, being commented on for example in the 1752 and 1771 editions of the *Dictionnaire Universel François et Latin,* where it is stated that marquetry has the defect of being subject to fading and becoming uniform in colour. Exposed to daylight, marquetry would have lost its colour very quickly, if not in weeks or months, then certainly within a few years. Eighteenth-century patrons and craftsmen went to great lengths to find ways of keeping the colour of their furniture. Among other suggestions, Roubo believed that the simple use of a polish to fill the grain would prevent the colour evaporating. Without understanding of the scientific properties of colour, this solution obviously proved unsuccessful. In fact, discolouration of the wood occurs only on its outermost exposed layer. A common method of reviving colour was to scrape away the outer layer, thereby revealing the vibrant colour beneath. The roll-top desk for Louis XV was delivered by Riesener to Versailles in 1769, and records

FIG 69

FIG 70

Figure 70
Modern reproduction of
a Boulle floral marquetry
panel made by Yannick
Chastang in 1995. Only
those species of woods
known to have been
available to Boulle were
used and eighteenth-
century recipes were used
to dye the stained woods.
The vase is made of blue-
painted horn imitating
lapis lazuli, as used in the
seventeenth century.

Figure 71
Detail of a porcelain
plaque mounted on a
Carlin work-table of *c.*1770.
The colours of eighteenth-
century marquetry were
designed to complement
such brightly coloured
painted compositions.
THE WALLACE COLLECTION,
INV. F327

tell us that it was scraped and polished to reinstate the original colours, by
Riesener himself, in 1776, 1777 and 1785. Only one year passed between the first
and second scraping, indicating how quickly the colours of the marquetry must
have deteriorated. Frequent repetition of this radical treatment is of course
likely to result in irrevocable loss of the marquetry itself. Each scraping or
sanding makes the veneer thinner and in most cases three or four such
treatments would be sufficient to remove all the surface decoration, exposing the
solid wood carcase. Nevertheless, the furniture was designed to be colourful and
any treatment, however damaging, was presumably regarded as worthwhile if it
revived the glory of the marquetry colours. The almost paper-thin condition of
the marquetry on the roll-top desk of Louis XV is today a particular problem for
conservators working at Versailles. Even where the wood carcase is not exposed
a veneer which is too thin will become saturated with glue and will become
unsightly. Scraping, unfortunately, all too often still is a common practice for
reviving original colour.

Marquetry was therefore designed with bright and vibrant colours and
marquetry seen today is only a pale reflection of the original intention. The
question we should perhaps ask is whether, given that the King admired his
colourful marquetry, he would still recognise and appreciate his pieces of
marquetry furniture which are on show at the Wallace Collection today? On the
other hand, would we, the modern visitor, accustomed by now to subtle tones of
brown, still enjoy the pieces if they could be restored to their vibrant colours?

FIG 71

FURTHER READING

Baarsen, R.
17th-century Cabinets, Rijksmuseum dossiers,
Amsterdam, 2000.

Bellaigue, G. de
*The James A. De Rothschild Collection At Waddesdon
Manor, Furniture, Clocks And Gilt Bronzes*
Fribourg, 1974.

Bellaigue, G. de
'Engravings and the French Eighteenth-century
Marqueteur', *The Burlington Magazine*
106 (1965), pp.240-50 (part 1);
107 (1965), pp.357-63 (part 2).

Dubon, D. and Dell, T.
*The Frick Collection, An Illustrated Catalogue, v,
Furniture, Italian & French,* New York, 1992
and Dell, T.
*The Frick Collection, An Illustrated Catalogue, VI,
Furniture And Gilt Bronzes, French,* New York, 1992.

Fleming, J., and Honour, H.
The Penguin Dictionary of Decorative Arts
London, 1989.

Guiffrey, J.
'Inventaire de Jean-François Oeben', *Nouvelles
Archives de l'Art Français,* VOL.XV 1899, pp.298-367.

Hayward, H
World Furniture, London, 1969.

Sir John Pope-Hennessy, Sir Francis Watson,
James Wheeler, Geoffrey Beard, et al.
The History of Furniture, 3rd edn, London, 1990.

Hughes, P.
The Wallace Collection, Catalogue of Furniture
London, 1996.

Lincoln, W. A.
The Art and Practice of Marquetry, London, 1971.

Mabille, G.
Arts et Techniques: Menuiserie-Ebénisterie, Paris, 1995.

Pereira Coutinho, M. I.
18th Century French Furniture, Calouste Gulbenkian
Museum, Lisbon, 1999.

Pradère, A.
*French Furniture Makers, The Art of the Ebéniste
from Louis XIV to the Revolution,* Paris, 1989.

Ramond, P.
Marquetry, Dourdan, 1989.

Ramond, P.
*Chefs d'Oeuvre des Marqueteurs I:
Des Origines à Louis XIV,*
Dourdan, 1994. English Edition, Sept 2001.
*Chefs d'Oeuvre des Marqueteurs II:
De la Régence à nos Jours*
Dourdan, 1994. English Edition, Sept 2001.
*Chefs d'Oeuvre des Marqueteurs III:
Marqueteurs d'Exception*
Dourdan, 1994. English Edition, Sept 2001.

Ronfort, J.-N.
'André-Charles Boulle: die Bronzearbeiten und seine Werkstatt im Louvre', in H. Ottomeyer and P. Pröschel (eds.), *Vergoldete Bronzen,* Munich, 1986, II, pp.459-520.

Roubo, A.-J.
Encyclopédie des arts de la Menuiserie, Paris 1772-74. Rep. Léonce Laget, Paris, 1977.

Samoyault, J. P.
André-Charles Boulle et sa Famille, Geneva, 1979.

Sargentson, C.
Merchants and Luxury Markets, London, 1996.

Verlet, P.
Le Mobilier Royal Français, VOL I, Paris, 1990.
Le Mobilier Royal Français, VOL II, Paris, 1992.
French Royal Furniture, VOL III, Paris, 1994.
Le Mobilier Royal Français, VOL IV, Paris, 1990.

Viaux-Locquin, J.
Les Bois d'Ebénisterie dans le Mobilier Français
Paris, 1997.

Walker, A.
The Encyclopaedia of Wood, London, 1989.

Watson, F. J. B
'A Note on French Marquetry and Oriental Lacquer'
The J. Paul Getty Museum Journal, 9 (1981), pp.157-66.

Wilmering, Antoine M. and Raggio Olga
The Gubbio Studiolo and its Conservation
The Metropolitan Museum of Art, New York, 1999.

Whitehead, J.
The French Interior In The Eighteenth Century, 1992.

Wolvesperges, T.
Le Meuble Français en Laque au XVIIIe Siècle
Paris, 2000.

Other Collections

Many of the examples of marquetry furniture discussed in this book may be seen in the Wallace Collection, London, which houses the most important collection of French 18th century decorative arts outside the Louvre. For readers wishing to see more French marquetry furniture, there follows a brief selection of some important collections.

United Kingdom ஒ

Waddesdon Manor (National Trust)
Aylesbury, Buckinghamshire

The Victoria and Albert Museum
London

The Royal Collection
Windsor Castle, Windsor
Buckingham Palace, London

United States ஒ

The Metropolitan Museum of Art
New York

The Frick Collection
New York

The Fine Arts Museums of San Francisco, M. H. de Young Memorial Museum
San Francisco

The J. Paul Getty Museum
Los Angeles

Henry E. Huntington Library and Art Gallery
San Marino

France ஒ

Musée du Louvre
Paris

Musée Nissim de Camondo
Paris

Musée Cognac-Jay
Paris

Musée Jacquemart-André
Paris

Musée National du Château de Versailles et de Trianon
Versailles

Germany ஒ

Residenzmuseum
Munich

Portugal ஒ

Museu Calouste Gulbenkian
Lisbon

Russia ஒ

State Hermitage Museum
St Petersburg